THE
REVENUE ACCELERATION
RULES

SHASHI UPADHYAY
KENT McCORMICK

THE
REVENUE
ACCELERATION
RULES

SUPERCHARGE SALES AND MARKETING

THROUGH

ARTIFICIAL INTELLIGENCE,
PREDICTIVE TECHNOLOGIES, AND
ACCOUNT-BASED STRATEGIES

WILEY

For general information on our other products and services or for technical support, please contact our Customer Care Department within the United States at (800) 762–2974, outside the United States at (317) 572–3993 or fax (317) 572–4002.

Wiley publishes in a variety of print and electronic formats and by print-on-demand. Some material included with standard print versions of this book may not be included in e-books or in print-on-demand. If this book refers to media such as a CD or DVD that is not included in the version you purchased, you may download this material at http://booksupport.wiley.com. For more information about Wiley products, visit www.wiley.com.

Library of Congress Cataloging-in-Publication Data:

Names: Upadhyay, Shashi, author. | McCormick, Kent (Product development
   consultant), author.
Title: The revenue acceleration rules : supercharge sales and marketing
   through artificial intelligence, predictive technologies and
   account-based strategies / by Shashi Upadhyay, Kent McCormick.
Description: Hoboken, New Jersey : John Wiley & Sons, Inc., [2018] | Includes
   index. |
Identifiers: LCCN 2018001026 (print) | LCCN 2018005178 (ebook) | ISBN
   9781119372066 (ePub) | ISBN 9781119372073 (ePDF) | ISBN 9781119371953
   (pbk.)
Subjects: LCSH: Industrial marketing. | Artificial intelligence.
Classification: LCC HF5415.1263 (ebook) | LCC HF5415.1263 .U63 2018 (print) |
   DDC 658.15/54–dc23
LC record available at https://lccn.loc.gov/2018001026

ISBN 9781119371953 (Hardcover)
ISBN 9781119372073 (ePDF)
ISBN 9781119372066 (ePub)

Printed in the United States of America

10 9 8 7 6 5 4 3 2 1

For Mira, Jayant, and Runi
—Shashi

To my family
—Kent

The authors' proceeds from this book will be donated to Doctors Without Borders (Medecins Sans Frontieres).

Contents

Acknowledgments

BUSINESS TO BUSINESS (B2B) marketing and sales technology has evolved at a breathtaking pace over the last decade. The convergence of ubiquitous data, artificial intelligence (AI), and account-based marketing (ABM) has created a perfect storm for practicing marketers and sales leaders. We were inspired to write this book by our customers who were asking for our help in navigating the ever-shifting landscape. In that sense, this is a collaborative effort of a very large group of people who have helped us develop these ideas, test them, and provide honest feedback—good or bad.

We have been very fortunate to have exceptional customers, who are all innovators and risk-takers. It started with John Smits, who gave us our first break as a company and has always prodded us to do better.

The original founding team at Lattice Engines included Andrew Schwartz and Michael McCarroll, who are still at Lattice a decade later. We have been inspired by their dedication, resilience, and commitment to the cause of making B2B revenue acceleration an analytical discipline. We were almost ten years too early to the party, but are thankful that it finally began.

Our investors, Doug Leone, Peter Sonsini, Mickey Arabelovic, Bob Rinek, Rami Rahal, Mir Arif, and Robert Heimann, have been a great source of advice on growing Lattice into a market leader. Alex Khein wrote us our first check and helped the company start.

We have benefited immensely from our conversations with Sharmila Shahani-Mulligan, who is arguably the best new-market creator in Silicon Valley. Judy Verses was the first marketing mentor for Shashi and helped foster his interest in applying hard-science techniques to B2B data. Peter Bisson, David Walrod, Rock Khanna, Carlos Kirjner, and Saf Yeboah were all early investors and advisors to the company as we left our comfortable corporate jobs and started Lattice.

We have been fortunate to have exemplary colleagues, each of whom has contributed directly or indirectly to this book through questions, ideas, and analytical work: Mike Alksninis, Barry Burns, Nipul Chokshi, Neil Cotton, Brett Dyer, Irina Egorova, Jean-Paul Gomes de Laroche, Taylor Grisham, Gregory Haardt, Scott Harralson, Brandt Hurd, Max Jacobson, Yoshino Kitajima, Greg Leibman, Luke McLemore, Feng Meng, Matthew Mesher, Bernard Nguyen, Sashi Nivarthi, Chitrang Shah, Imran Ulla, Nelson Wiggins, Jason Williams, Matt Wilson, Jerry Wish, Mimy Wraspir, and Yunfeng Yang.

Caitlin Ridge has played a central role in the creation of this book. She has a unique ability to take half-crafted ideas and turn them into life with words. In addition to performing her duties as the director of corporate marketing, she led the team to create content, meet deadlines, and keep our commitments. This book would not have happened with Caitlin's dedication, work ethic, and raw horsepower.

As we found out, writing a book while growing a company is not an easy task. We appreciate the help and support of our families, not just in writing this book, but throughout the process of building Lattice. This book is dedicated to them.

About the Authors

SHASHI UPADHYAY, PH.D., is the chief executive officer of Lattice Engines. Shashi is responsible for advancing Lattice's vision to deliver the power of AI to sales and marketing organizations. His unique background as a physicist turned McKinsey partner drove the founding of Lattice.

Shashi has written extensively about the impact of Artificial Intelligence on business. Outside of technology, Shashi is a warm-water surfer, lapsed amateur boxer, and a voracious nonfiction reader. He has also served as an advisor to Amar Chitra Katha, the leading children's publisher in India, and Halo, a neuroscience company.

Shashi holds an undergraduate degree from the Indian Institute of Technology at Kanpur and a Ph.D. in physics from Cornell University.

KENT MCCORMICK, PH.D., is the vice president of innovation and data science at Lattice Engines. Kent is responsible for setting product direction and deployment activities. Before founding Lattice Engines, Kent served as director of business operations at EMC. In this role, he led pricing and operational analytics for all of EMC. Before this, Kent was a consultant at McKinsey & Company, working with Fortune 500 companies on product development and solving sales and marketing business problems.

Kent received a Ph.D. in physics from the University of California, Berkeley, and before that a dual-degree in physics and mathematics from Rice University.

Introduction

IMAGINE A WORLD with 1-to-1 marketing. Your current and prospective suppliers and vendors understand your business needs, so when you open your inbox in the morning it's not a flood of random offers. Instead, your email brings up a carefully curated, small list of personalized offers that you're actually happy to receive. You know that what they're offering will be relevant to your business, and you know it will be worth your time to spend a few minutes perusing the content they've sent. The information they've sent you is not only entertaining but it's engaging, and it will solve some of the pain points you're facing with your organization.

In this world, the CMO is a master orchestrator of the customer experience, using data-rich technology to truly understand customers, so contextualized, personalized content is sent to the correct set of target contacts at the right accounts at the right time. Sounds like heaven, right?

Unfortunately, that is not the world we live in today. We live in a world in which an abundance of email and advertising spam has taken over our inboxes like a poorly executed coup d'état in a banana republic. The spam is in charge, but no one is happy with the end result.

With the growth of generic, impersonal information flowing to prospects out of every company in the B2B world, engagement rates are down across the board for digital programs. In an attempt to block out the spam, people are turning away from any email,

1

advertising, or content that comes their way. And no one can blame them, with the flood of generic information being flung at people today it's a wonder we haven't all gone crazy. To deal with the flood we ignore 90 percent of our inboxes and turn a blind eye to the advertising that covers the borders of any websites we visit. And it's not just marketing teams who should be blamed for this; there has been an uptick of generic, spammy email from sales teams as well. All this technology has done the exact opposite of what it was supposed to do—create intimacy with our customers.

At the same time that this spam coup took place and we all lost control of our inboxes, CMOs at most major companies were rightly given more responsibility and more budget. Companies realize that marketing plays a major role in their pipeline creation and acceleration, and marketing organizations are becoming more horizontal so they can organize the messaging and activities that take place across their business. Marketing teams responded to this challenge by building more robust technology stacks to address their new responsibilities, and the marketing technology industry responded by growing at exponential rates in order to meet the technological demands of a new crop of data-savvy marketers.

However, despite the increase in technology, most marketing teams are seeing declining engagement results that they're unable to explain. Without a clear way to explain the impact their teams have on revenues, CMOs will lose the responsibility they've been handed. This issue first came up when marketing teams started adding so many more tools to their technology stack. Many of the new solutions were built in a way that they inherently created their own silos of data, meaning that marketing teams who added fifteen new tools over the past year also added fifteen new data silos that they had to try to reconcile. This means there is no one place where marketing teams can go to see a clear picture and understand their customer and prospect accounts.

There is a way to cure this growing problem of spam and impersonal content being thrown at every person in a database, and a way for CMOs to start achieving the kinds of measurable results they know their teams are capable of. In this book, we argue that the solution to this problem is two-fold, and we'll delve into the specifics of how to start. First, companies need to integrate their data into one platform so they have a single view of all customer and prospects' insights, and second, they need to use artificial intelligence (AI) and machine learning to drive analytics-based campaign actions that will move themselves closer to 1-to-1 marketing.

In addition to helping companies start on this path toward targeted, 1-to-1 marketing, we'll discuss the nuances that exist for different business models, including: (1) companies currently largely dependent on inbound leads; (2) companies that are transitioning from inbound leads to an account-centric focus; (3) companies that only have direct sales with little marketing support; and (4) companies that rely more heavily on channel sales.

We want readers to know that you're not alone—this is a problem most organizations are facing today. The solution is already out there, and the best companies have realized that data and insight about customers are the foundation on which any 1:1 program has to be built. They have started to put the technologies, the processes, and the metrics in place to take advantage of all the data they are gathering, so they can engage with their customers at the right time with the right message.

A final word before you dive in. If you're a data-driven marketer and really want to understand the impact of data and AI on marketing, read the whole book and pay special attention to Chapters 3 and 6. If you're just curious about the space and not looking for an in-depth understanding of the data framework behind AI platforms, you can skim those two chapters and focus your attention on the rest of the book.

1

The CMO's Challenge

"The aim of marketing is to understand a customer so well that the product or service fits him and sells itself."

—*Peter Drucker*

CHIEF MARKETING OFFICERS (CMOs) have the toughest job in the C-suite today. They stand at the intersection of a set of convergent changes, never encountered before in the history of business-to-business (B2B) marketing. They are being asked to digitize the front office, take ownership of customer data, support sales with leads, find new market opportunities, and explain the impact of their spending on revenue, all at once.

Unlike in other functions, most CMOs today have not had the opportunity to gradually ease into the role. There is nothing about their training that could have prepared them. There are no marketing academies yet, companies that trained and graduated large numbers of well-trained, competent marketers. As a result, most CMOs take a varied path through their careers, and it is not unusual to find people who started out in marketing events, inside sales, or product management in a CMO role. What's common across these paths? Nothing except the ability to be a good generalist and to learn quickly on the job.

Business-to-business CMOs have an especially hard task because, unlike their business-to-consumer (B2C) counterparts, they are measured by the success of a function they don't control—the sales team. For a very long time, B2B marketers have been subservient to the needs of the sales team. The wide availability of data and techniques for generating it is starting to change that, but there is a long way to go.

As if this were not enough, the constant technology shocks and hype-cycles further make it hard for CMOs to make any decisions. There are over five thousand marketing technologies available at the time this book is being written, according to Scott Brinker's Marketing Technology Landscape Supergraphic (see Figure 1.2). Not only does the CMO have to find people who understand these technologies, but the bar is even higher as these technologies need to be selected, integrated, and deployed into existing or new workflows. The very fact that most marketing organizations already use seventeen different technologies on average shows how hard the problem is.

All of this creates a credibility problem for the CMO. We have often found CMOs struggling with making the kind of impact they would like to. Far too often, their CEOs are unhappy with the gap between expectation and reality. Why can't we move faster? Why can't we find more leads? Why aren't we growing current customers? Why can't we identify new markets? What did we get for all the program money we spend? And why can't you hold on to anyone on your team? No wonder then that CMO tenure is at its lowest in history, according to research from executive search firm Spencer Stuart.

On the bright side, if the CMO could answer all these questions, why does one need a CEO? In fact, we will argue later that the CMO role will become the best training ground to be the CEO of any B2B organization. But we are getting ahead of ourselves here. Let's start with what a marketing organization is supposed to do.

The Fundamental Goals of Marketing

Peter Drucker, one of the modern gurus of management, defined marketing's primary role as understanding the customer so well that the product would sell itself. In the real world, there is never one customer, nor even a few major segments. In fact, the real promise of modern marketing is that a brand can interact with each cus-tomer on his or her terms, create a unique experience just for that customer, and engage, inform, and educate each customer through the process.

This was the core idea behind the seminal book *The One to One Future* by Don Peppers and Martha Rogers. The book was more than twenty years ahead of its time, as the technology to implement these ideas were not available in 1996. That is now changing rapidly.

The goal of a modern marketing organization is three-fold:

1. Understand what's unique about every customer,
2. Craft a tailored customer experience for each of them, at scale, and
3. Lead them through a journey that will create the most value for customers and for the provider as a consequence.

Why is this so hard?

The Deconstruction of B2B

B2B was a simpler place a decade ago. Marketers managed the brand, created product brochures, and ran events. Sales reps did everything from prospecting to closing to expanding the customer base. Then specialization happened, and companies found it more expedient to split up the work across separate mini-functions. New groups emerged in the front office: the demand-gen team, the SDRs, the closers, the customer success team, and so on. Over time, even these specialties continue to break down into narrower silos. It is not uncommon in most organizations to have different people responsible for email campaigns, ads, videos, social media, and more.

This kind of specialization creates a huge challenge for CMOs, because they can't be experts in everything and have to rely on a large group of people who know more than they do (see Figure 1.1).

The App Explosion

The deconstruction of the front office has been further accelerated by vendors. Each role now has its own app. There are apps for posting videos, tracking social media, . . . and even apps to manage other apps. You would think that marketers would be happy with this plethora of choice. Instead they are suffering from a curse of abundance. As Scott Brinker has pointed out on his MarTech blog, this abundance creates an inability to digest all this innovation and freezes marketers into place, where they can't even do the obvious things well.

The explosion of apps creates a secondary problem in that each of them creates its own data, has its own middleware, and is focused on its own set of reports. See Figure 1.2 for some of the possibilities.

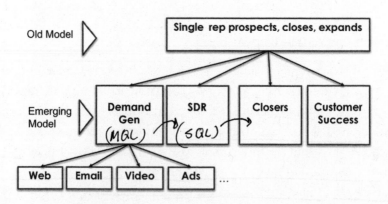

Figure 1.1   The Old Model vs. the Emerging Model of Marketing

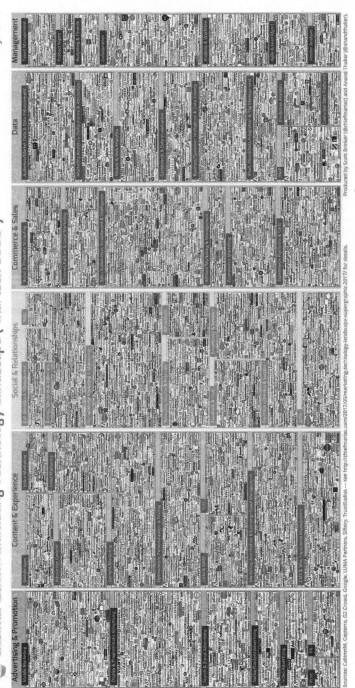

Figure 1.2 Marketing Technology Landscape

Source: © LUMA Partners LLC 2013. Used with permission.

Since most of the apps are solving a narrow problem, they come with proximate metrics. For example, an oft-used metric is percentage of opened emails. While you would expect this has something to do with the ultimate metric, revenue generated, the connection is not so clear. Clever marketers have been known to increase the percentage-opened metric by using images and videos that entertain but have nothing to do with the product. There is higher engagement but no additional positive impact on the ultimate goal of more revenue.

Specialization Sustains Vanity Metrics

Deconstruction of the marketing organization and the spread of apps is not the whole story, however. The real problem is that each app generates its own data and focuses on a narrow set of metrics that may or may not have to do with revenue generation. Vanity metrics are proxies for the ultimate goals of revenue and margin growth. These metrics create the impression and comfort of being metrics-driven, yet they have neither explanatory nor predictive value.

Imagine a board meeting where the CMO and the CSO are presenting. While the CSO talks about sales and pipeline growth, which anyone can relate to, the CMO talks about increase in visitors to the website and the click-through rates of the latest email campaign. Everyone is left wondering whether the CMO has a real handle on the revenue generation problem (Figure 1.3).

Since the vendors aren't doing anything to connect the impact of their favored metrics to revenue and margin growth, the job is left to the marketing team to figure out how to connect their tactics and programs to sales growth.

The unique aspect of the CMO's role is that they have a thousand instruments, yet only one metric that the CEO cares about. This metric is "total opportunity created." Therefore, this is a classic optimization problem: set up your factory from a choice of hundreds of technologies and providers so that you can maximize "total opportunity created."

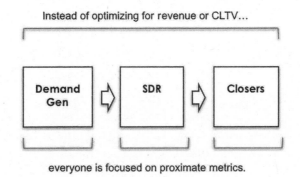

Figure 1.3 Focusing on the Wrong Metrics

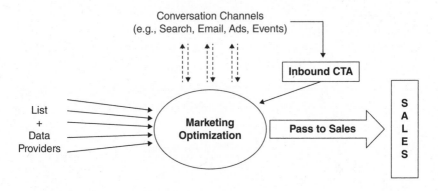

Figure 1.4 Revenue Conversion Channels

Each of these technologies generates a massive amount of data that is either useless or confusing from the perspective of creating opportunities. For example, take the metric of open-rates for emails. Clearly, a low open-rate is bad news, but is a high open-rate necessarily good news? You can always increase open-rate by targeting a very narrow segment or creating entertaining content that has nothing to do with your offer or positioning in the market (Figure 1.4).

Too much of marketing technology stack is sub-optimized in the sense that it focuses on these proximate goals and metrics, instead of on the ultimate goal of maximizing opportunity and revenue creation.

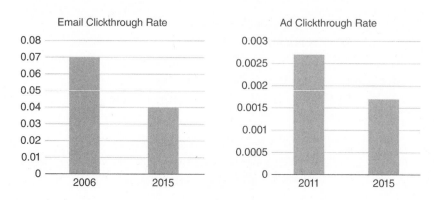

Figure 1.5   Comparison of Clickthrough Rates

Deconstruction = Depersonalization

Unfortunately, the net result of all these trends is a movement away from 1:1. That's right, the net effect of marketing automation and all the ad tech unleashed in the world has been a drive toward less engagement, less personalization, more spam, and generally a worse customer experience (Figure 1.5).

What's a CMO to Do?

It is against this backdrop that two trends have arisen simultaneously: ABM and AI, in order to address the declining engagement rate problem. Let's start with ABM:

Account-Based Marketing

Sales leaders are used to thinking in terms of accounts. You will never hear them say, "I just closed a deal with Joe Schultz"; instead they will take pride in closing the deal at Apple or IBM or wherever it is that Joe Shultz works. Marketers on the other hand tend to think in terms of contacts, leads, and people, because a "lead" is a person. Contacts versus accounts is a source of tremendous friction inside organizations.

The myriad of technologies that the CMO deploys don't follow a consistent schema or definition in terms of how they define accounts, leads, and so on. As a result, all the work of mapping data, matching it, deduping it, attributing it correctly, and then trying to derive insights from it—all of it falls on the CMO's organization, which is then not well-suited to execute because the data is unusable.

It's partly in recognition of the waste created by the undifferentiated "spray and pray" approaches and the cost of backing into an account-based view for sales that practitioners of lead-based marketing have started to shift toward ABM. More on this later.

What Is ABM?

Sales has always been account-based; *marketing* must transition to ABM from lead-based programs. Opportunity is really at the intersection of marketing and sales, helping to manage what goes to sales, the mix of inbound leads, scored leads, and outbounds (unresponsive target markets). Account-based marketing and sales (ABM&S) starts with target accounts, creates campaigns for these, sets up nurture, and helps to manage what goes to sales.

- ABM is the right way to do things. It is the B2B equivalent of 1:1 marketing.
- ABM saves money by taking focus away from un-interested accounts.
- ABM puts sales and marketing on the same page and integrates sales activities (such as territory planning) with marketing activities (like field marketing).
- A full ABMS solution will cover everything from modeling/ target setting, campaign creation, threshold setting for passing to sales, content, portfolio management across different segments/models, and reporting and measurement of value.

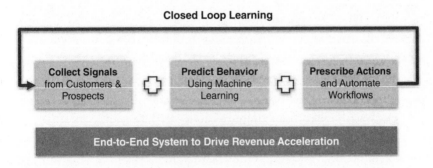

Figure 1.6   Closed Loop Learning

Artificial Intelligence and Machine Learning

Machine learning is a relatively new discipline of computer science. It helps software learn through examples. AI includes machine learning as well as a few other methods like computer vision and search. Artificial intelligence (AI) lurks behind consumer applications, often without the end-user's knowledge. From identifying images to recommending friends to serving the right ad, web-scale data has rendered many old algorithms (e.g., neural networks) potent and capable of beating humans at similar tasks (Figure 1.6).

In the world of marketing and sales, the equivalent of the new AI are predictive marketing and sales applications. For tasks like targeting accounts, micro-segmenting audiences, and matching optimal actions, they are starting to take over the workloads of marketers and inside sales professionals.

Opportunity for the CMO

The combination of ABM and AI offers a magic bullet to the CMO. AI helps discover targets that are likely to convert, and therefore move marketers back to the 1:1 world. ABM helps create a common language between sales and marketing and creates further alignment. And since AI is based on data, it makes it a lot easier for the CMO to talk in terms of real numbers and hard metrics. Moreover, given the very nature of AI, it needs fewer human experts, and will take over the mundane data tasks that marketers hate and give them the bandwidth to focus on creative aspects of their business processes.

In the rest of the book we will cover how these two trends are transforming marketing, aligning them with sales, and help you accelerate your revenue generation by using them in concert. First, we'll look at how critical having clean, accurate data is to these processes and how to set your data-foundation correctly.

2

ABM and AI

As DISCUSSED IN Chapter 1, account-based marketing (ABM) flips the traditional funnel on its head. In contrast to traditional lead generation, ABM starts by identifying those accounts you want to convert (focus on quality versus quantity). Everything flows from this list of targets. Messages, content, and offers are tailored to those accounts and personas within accounts. Finally, marketing and sales executes tactics designed to convert, not just capture names or fill lead-forms.

Most companies have been doing account-based marketing for years. However, their efforts have been targeted at their top fifty to one hundred accounts because of the resources required for selecting target accounts, researching their key challenges, developing customized offers, and driving campaigns in a coordinated way between sales and marketing. Scaling this approach to the entire account base has proven challenging.

B2B buyers are savvier than ever—armed with more choices, more information, and an expectation for a "B2C-like experience" when it comes to interactions with brands. We are seeing three key trends that set up some fundamental challenges for B2B marketers:

1. **Buyers are increasingly self-directed.** According to research from the Corporate Executive Board (https://www.cebglobal.com/marketing-communications/digital-evolution.html), B2B buyers do not contact suppliers directly until 57 percent of the purchase process is complete. Just as they're empowered to do so in their personal lives, B2B buyers are conducting research online before engaging with brands. Brand marketers are thus challenged with finding and reaching buyers at each stage of the buying process—before they raise their hands, after they raise their hands, and after they engage with sales.

2. **B2B buying has become a team sport.** Up to seventeen people are involved in an enterprise buying decision (that's up from ten just two years ago). Brands must find and engage with all the relevant parties—economic buyers, decision makers, and influencers—within the accounts they wish to convert to customers.

3. **Buyers expect relevance and insights.** According to a study by SiriusDecisions (https://www.siriusdecisions.com/blog/its-not-content–its-a-lack-of-buyer-insights-thats-the-problem), up to 80 percent of B2B content goes unused. It's not that buyers are averse to content—it's that much of it is generic, irrelevant, and not actionable. Seventy-five percent of business executives surveyed said they were willing to read unsolicited marketing materials if they were relevant to their industry and role (per research from ITSMA [https://www.itsma.com/category/article/page/38/]).

In short, B2B brands must have relevant and meaningful conversations with multiple individuals across multiple channels at each stage of the buying process. Unfortunately, traditional broad-based lead generation is not working. Is it any wonder that less than 1 percent of leads turn into revenue?

While ABM is certainly not new (companies have been doing it for years), thanks to new technologies, companies are poised to take advantage of ABM at greater scale. Just as the B2C space has had the one-to-one personalization movement, account-based marketing has been establishing more mindshare among B2B marketers. There are various definitions of ABM, but we've taken the standard SiriusDecisions definition and summarized it as follows:

In traditional lead generation, marketers will typically lead the buyer down the traditional marketing and sales funnel we are all aware of. The goal is to capture as many "leads" as possible—without regard to how likely those leads are to convert (that is left to sales in most organizations as part of the qualification process). Marketers start with their own company's value proposition—on which all messages, content, and offers will be based. They'll then execute tactics that "get the word out" as broadly as possible in hopes of capturing as many leads as possible.

Benefits of ABM

Account-based marketing drives business benefits in various ways:

1. **It aligns sales and marketing.** Unlike traditional lead-based marketing, where marketing cares about "getting leads" and sales cares about "closing accounts," ABM revolves around marketing and selling to a set of accounts (or segments) that are jointly defined by sales and marketing.
2. **It relies on a heavily personalized approach.** Personalized content delivers five to eight times ROI on marketing spend and can lift sales by 10 percent or more.
3. **It applies not just to finding and landing net new customers,** but also to expanding your relationships with existing customers as well.

Scaling ABM Requires AI

Most companies have been doing account-based marketing for years. Their efforts are targeted at their top fifty to one hundred accounts because of the resources required for selecting target accounts, researching their key challenges, developing customized offers, and driving campaigns in a coordinated way between sales and marketing.

As the marketing technology stack has evolved, however, companies are able to use artificial intelligence everywhere to automate and scale ABM to all their accounts, independent of target market size.

AI platforms provide the data and insights needed to execute on the sophisticated segmentation and personalization required for successful ABM programs. They bring several capabilities to bear.

360-Degree View of Prospects and Customers

AI based insight-platforms provide you the ability to look at all the data you already have about your prospects and customers—for example, marketing automation, sales interactions (CRM), support tickets, transactions, product usages, and so on.

Additionally, AI platforms add in external data you may not have about your prospects and customers (or easily capture)—for example, growth rates, funding information, credit risk data, technographic data (what technologies they are using), and so forth.

AI platforms combine all your internal and external data, bringing thousands of data points around each prospect or customer that you have.

Big Data Processing and Machine Learning

With AI, you can harness the power of big data processing and machine learning to create predictive models easily for scoring customers and prospects based on how likely they are to buy, what they're likely to buy, and when. You also get a prioritized list of attributes about your ideal buyer that you can use to enhance your personas.

Ability to Operationalize Insights

Finally, AI platforms make the predictive scores and account-level insights and data available in real time to your ad platforms, marketing automation systems, and CRM systems so you can drive the right campaigns and end-user experiences.

The rest of this book will provide a framework and examples of how companies can use AI and AI to scale their account-based marketing programs, thereby driving increased revenue for their companies.

Winning Plays for Scaling Your ABM Programs

AI vendors now make it easy for sales and marketing to take advantage of advanced data science without needing to turn to data scientists, Ph.D.s, and data specialists. Companies can execute on account-based marketing on a larger scale—whether it's targeting a greater number of accounts (beyond the traditional top fifty or top one hundred accounts), driving install-base customer retention and revenue (cross-sell/up-sell), or marketing to segments of accounts.

You can use four key plays to scale your account-based marketing programs using AI:

1. Target your high-value accounts.
2. Tailor content and messages for maximum relevance.
3. Execute tactics designed to convert (not just move leads through the funnel).
4. Measure impact and iterate.

Next we will look at each of these plays in further detail. Figure 2.1 summarizes the key points for each play:

FIT	How closely they resemble your ideal customer in terms of firmographic attributes. It tells you "What's the likelihood this account will become my customer?"
LIFETIME VALUE	How much revenue each account is most likely to contribute. It tells you "How much is this account likely to spend with me?"

Figure 2.1   Summary of Key Points

Target Your High-Value Accounts

The foundation of any ABM program is having a defined target segment or list of companies to proactively pursue. Traditionally, the process of identifying a list of targets has been based on guesswork or limited data. For example, "We sell to companies based in the Northeast with five to twenty-five employees." Alternatively, "Sales comes up with a list based on their experience and gives it to Marketing."

As a result, marketers wind up buying lists of leads or running broad-based inbound programs that may target the right person, but the wrong company. This is equal to "spray and pray" marketing that may yield a lot of leads (great for marketing), but not actually converted revenue (not so great for sales and the company in general).

AI helps you do three things so that you are targeting your highest value accounts.

Score and Prioritize Your Accounts   Your AI platform will score the targets in your account universe based on how closely they resemble your customers. There are two elements to the score (Figure 2.1); you can combine these two elements using the framework below to classify your target universe into "A" accounts, "B" accounts, and so on.

The "A" accounts become your top-tier targets, closely followed by "B" accounts. These are the accounts you will proactively target as part of your ABM effort. This becomes your starting point for

T.A.M.

creating a targeted and engaging strategy for the accounts you'll be proactively going after.

Alternatively, "C" and "D" accounts may not be part of your targeted outreach. If you're running inbound lead generation programs, you may capture some "fish" from these accounts, in which case, score their level of engagement with your inbound programs (either using AI or standard rules-based scoring found in marketing automation platforms), and put them into the appropriate nurture programs.

Identify Accounts That Are "In Market"   Upon creating a prioritized target list, you want to see which accounts are "in market," that is, accounts that are actively looking for your solution. Typically, you'll be leveraging third-party intent data and combining that with data you already have in your marketing automation.

You can use these insights to decide whether you want to have Sales directly reach out to a prospect (a high-scoring prospect that has viewed multiple webinars and visited your pricing page is most likely further down the buying journey—and so would likely be receptive to a sales call).

Build Your Account and Contact Database   Now that you have a scored list of "A" and "B" accounts, you should add the following to your database so that you are ready to execute on your outreach campaigns against these accounts.

Account profile information   This includes attributes used in your ideal customer profile. This data will be useful when it comes to segmentation and targeting for your campaigns.

Contacts   Needless to say, you need a list of quality contacts for your campaigns as well. Typically, you will target specific job titles/ functions in the list of "A" and "B" accounts you've just created.

In general, your AI vendor should be able to source one or both of these. You should also be able to leverage your existing contacts provider for the contacts data.

mfgR → Knows target
SaaS → Knows "company type" (profile = IcP)

Create Relevant Messages and Content

Account-based marketing relies on customized messages, content, and offers to be most effective. Most likely marketers already are creating buyer personas to try to identify the key characteristics of your buyers, including their firmographics, key pain points and challenges, where they tend to "hang out," and other data.

AI enables you to super-charge these personas and find a deep understanding of your buyers in this way:

Identify Key Buyer Attributes   As part of any targeting exercise, Sales, Marketing, and line of business executives will have assumptions around the key characteristics of your ideal buyers. More often than not, these assumptions include things like "annual revenue > 100M" or "employees > 50" or "industry = finance, high tech, or manufacturing."

AI enables you to dig deeper by bringing in thousands of data points about the accounts and buyers you are targeting. These data points can be a mix of data you already have as well as other publicly available data.

While not all may be relevant or useful for targeting purposes, predictive models can also tell you what the top ten to fifteen attributes are so that you can use them for segmentation purposes.

Enrich Personas with Account-Level Insights   Buyer personas are the foundation of any targeted marketing strategy. Done right, personas are a very powerful tool for really understanding your buyers, the questions they ask, and the journey they take in order to identify and solve their problems. Account-based marketing relies on account-level insights to add important business context to your buyer personas and provide a true 360-degree view of your targets.

The point here is that, while you are targeting companies, you are still selling to people—in fact, you're typically selling to a committee in B2B. The key is to identify the different titles/job functions involved and understand the people's roles in the buying process. For instance, if you're selling marketing automation software, the CMO may well be the economic buyer while the vice president of operations may be a key influencer/ evaluator. IT, on the other hand, may be responsible for vetting a solution's compliance with organizational security and privacy policies.

Note that in small businesses, often a single person may wear multiple hats. In that instance, you should be sure to adapt your personas appropriately.

Segment Your Targets to Customize Your Message   Now that you have your database of accounts and contacts along with your enriched buyer personas, you can segment the database and create tailored messages for each segment. Ultimately, as part of your ABM effort, you're reaching out to your prioritized list of "A" and "B" accounts. With more granular segmentation, you have the opportunity to have more relevant conversations with these accounts.

While traditionally account-level segmentation is limited to the standard firmographic information (location, annual revenue, employee size), companies leveraging predictive marketing are able to tap into thousands of additional account-level attributes and signals for segmentation purposes.

Execute Tactics for Conversion

With ABM, marketing's focus shifts from driving "more leads" (lead quantity) to "engaging with the right accounts" (lead quality). Marketing tactics must change as well—so they are more focused on engaging with the right accounts, at the right time, via the right channel.

Use tactics that allow for sophisticated segmentation. Sales and marketing have a myriad of tactics up their sleeve when it comes to doing customer outreach. For ABM, however, it is important to leverage those tactics that most allow for sophisticated segmentation, targeting, and personalization. (S.T.P)

2) Monitor targets in real time for buying signals, engagement, and intent. In addition to proactive outreach, you want to monitor your target accounts to see whether any of the important attributes (a) have changed, (b) have engaged with your inbound programs, or (c) have expressed intent on the web.

Triggers + Rules

For example, an IT services provider had discovered that companies who were most likely to convert had just recently hired a CIO. As soon as a company on their target account list had hired a CIO, a personalized email was sent to that CIO along with an alert to the sales rep for that account.

3) Contextualize sales conversations with shared insights. The wealth of predictive insights about your targets should be shared with your sales team as well. As a sales rep or SDR reaches out to an account, they need to do research to understand the account, their business challenges, how your brand can help address those challenges, and so forth.

AI platforms enable marketers to share these insights in a very easy and consumable way:

First, bring these insights into your CRM system. Sales reps live in CRM, so make the additional insights available there.

Second, it's not just about sharing the account scores, but the underlying attributes that show why the account would be a good customer (Did they just hire a new CIO? Are they big users of a specific complementary technology?). See Figure 2.2 for an example of what such a dashboard could look like.

Finally, help sales easily integrate these insights into their conversations. Predictive marketing platforms provide the ability to craft templated "talking points," which enable marketers to integrate the account score, predictive attributes, value prop information about the solutions being proposed, products already purchased, and so forth in an easy to understand dashboard.

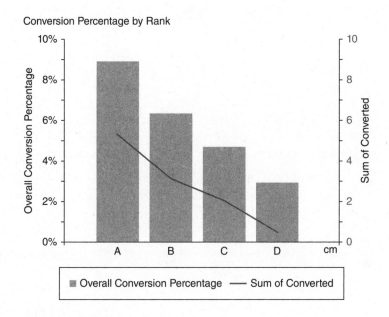

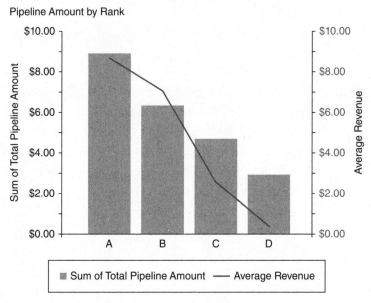

Figure 2.2   Sample Dashboard

Measure Impact

In contrast to traditional lead management, ABM strives to put sales and marketing on the same page with respect to success metrics. AI platforms enable you to measure the impact of your sales and marketing efforts on your business in three ways.

Measure progress in real time. While account-based marketing aligns sales and marketing on revenue impact metrics, you can use a combination of AI, marketing automation, and account-based marketing platforms to monitor progress in real time. Figure 2.2 suggests key metrics you should be able to measure in real time to evaluate progress of your ABM program.

Evaluate program performance. Measuring ABM program performance means looking at two things:

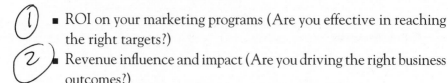

- ROI on your marketing programs (Are you effective in reaching the right targets?)
- Revenue influence and impact (Are you driving the right business outcomes?)

You can typically use a combination of AI, marketing automation, and CRM to create these reports. Figure 2.2 provides an example dashboard that shows conversion and pipeline metrics broken out by "A" accounts, "B" accounts, and so on.

Enable front-line sales performance management. A key best practice we've observed is providing these reports and dashboards to front-line sales managers so they can use them to coach reps on their teams. It is powerful indeed to be able to show how a particular rep is engaging on her target accounts—if she's not following up on her "A" accounts, managers could probe into the reasons why—Is she unclear as to what value prop would resonate with those accounts? Is he having trouble getting access to the right people at those accounts?

Summary

The B2B buying process has irrevocably changed and will continue to do so. Buyers are more in control than ever, and it is up to brands to engage with them earlier in the buying cycle rather than waiting for them to raise their hands. At the same time, buyers are being inundated with content, so brands need to provide relevant, insightful, and actionable content in order to stand out. This is what account-based marketing is all about and leading marketers have found that predictive marketing leads to ABM success in a much more efficient way.

Identify and prioritize your target accounts and understand what messages and content will resonate, rather than starting with your organization/value proposition and targeting personas. Be targeted in your outreach, using channels and tactics that allow for segmentation and personalization. Account-based marketing is proving to be an effective mindshift and approach for SMBs and enterprises alike to grow revenue, accelerate deals, and improve conversions.

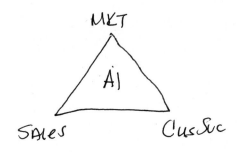

3

Data as the Foundation for ABM

ONE OF THE hardest things to get right for ABM is the level of effort to invest in data and analytics assets. Organizations often swing between the extremes of massive "data lake" projects designed to pull in all available enterprise data and the need to hack together account and contact lists just to get through the next campaign. In this chapter, you will see how to organize your data investments to gain the maximum impact for your ABM efforts. We begin with a five-step analytical process and then discuss some common pitfalls that can derail ABM projects.

Five Steps to a Robust Data Foundation

Like other projects, analytic efforts benefit from careful oversight. It can be difficult to balance efforts between the need to improve the analytics and the need to get something done quickly. As with all complex software integration efforts, the best practice is to develop the capability iteratively and to drive hard to complete a full cycle from data to revenue as quickly as possible. This provides a common understanding of the challenges, risks, and opportunities for the team and helps to provide a reference point for the larger organization. In that spirit, we

31

recommend following a structured process to make sure that key items are done, while setting an aggressive schedule with hard deadlines to keep the team accountable. Here are the five main steps for getting the data foundation right for ABM and AI driven initiatives:

1. Bound project objectives and scope with available data.
2. Consolidate and align historic data.
3. Build creative segments and audiences using AI.
4. Execute campaigns against AI-assisted segments and audiences.
5. Measure results on revenue, opportunity, and engagement metrics.

Bound Project Objectives and Scope with Available Data

The purpose of this phase is to set up the project both for success and for subsequent learning. Success requires that the objective be obtainable—in terms of the analytical operations and the data availability, but also in terms of the clarity of the desired outcome. The idea is to chart a course that reflects the spirit of the high-level business objective while recognizing the constraints imposed by existing data assets. The activity in this phase is not strictly linear, but instead consists of interplay among the following tasks to converge on a workable approach:

- Set a business objective.
- Define a target event.
- Translate the business objective into calculable events.
- Decide on the process step and execution channel.

Set a Business Objective   It is often assumed that the business objective is either too obvious or too trivial to warrant a discussion. But if the objective is not clear, it just pushes the analysis and decision making to later phases of the project, when it is harder to adjust course. Executives miss an opportunity to add their perspectives on market priorities when they skip this step. Moreover, a lack of clarity on the objective often indicates that more strategic thinking needs to be done. For example, a diagnostic project may be needed to understand where there is the most falloff in the sales and marketing pipeline. Or perhaps there is a lack of understanding of the incremental value of investments in marketing channels and events.

When a gap exists at the level of the business objective, projects are rarely successful. Writing down the objective often serves to clarify it. Even if the objective does shift over the course of the project, there is a shared understanding of what was expected from the original analytic process.

Good business objectives speak to at least a few of the following:

- What is the target market for the objective? *WHO*
- Which go-to-market model is to be employed? *HOW*
- What are the business metrics and timing of interest? *WHAT*
- What is the hypothesis about how execution can improve to meet this objective? *WHY*

Define a "Target Event" A target event is a measurable, historical fact that you can identify in your data. The fact may be the occurrence or non-occurrence of an outcome. It may also be a quantitative measure (such as revenue). In either case you should be able to identify the account or contact (or sometimes both) associated with the event, and you should be able to justify that the historical event corresponds to the business objective for the analysis. Table 3.1 illustrates some of example objectives and their corresponding events.

Good choices for events have the following properties:

- They occur reasonably frequently in the historical data.
- They measure a particular aspect of a business process.
- They can be determined from data that you have.
- They are expected to recur in a way that relates to the business objective.

Table 3.1   Sample Objectives and Events

Business Objective	Event	Comments
Grow revenue	Conversion of engaged contacts to sales qualified leads	■ One of many possible events ■ Event only addresses one part of the business process
Sell a new product to existing customers	Existing customers that purchased similar new products within six months of their introduction	■ No historical data if the product is new ■ Selecting similar products requires market insight ■ Event will necessarily differ from measurement
Reduce churn	Existing customers with more than 20 percent decline in month-on-month logins	■ Logins are a proxy for customer desire to renew

For the example of selling a new product, it is not possible to find an exact match in the historical data since the product is new. Nevertheless, there are a few ways to make progress. The approach in the example is to use historical data on similar product introductions. Alternatively, you could build a profile of an early adopter for the target market segment for the product and then define the event as membership in that category. Both approaches can succeed. Without the benefit of experience, you won't be able to make that judgment. The best approach is to pick a reasonable path and move forward to gain experience from executing a full process.

When considering a high-level objective such as "grow revenue," many candidate events potentially contribute to the goal. One tactic is to focus on the weakest link in your existing demand generation process and to structure an event that can be used to improve the effectiveness of that step. In the table, it is assumed that sales engagement with marketing leads is poor because of historically low-performing leads. By identifying the types of leads that the sales team is willing to engage, the overall process becomes more efficient. In addition, the sales team follows up on leads more diligently and their efforts are focused only on the leads with the highest potential.

Translate the Business Objective into Calculable Attributes Almost every business would like to deploy their salespeople to accounts with committed budgets, a felt need for their product, and the desire to close business in the current quarter. Usually that kind of information is not available or requires cost-prohibitive research. Potential customers may not even know, because they haven't framed their own requirements in sufficient detail. Because of these limitations, you may be forced to represent your business objective in other, more data-centric ways.

Another kind of gap can arise when information that is available is not organized in a way that allows you to correlate it to the objective you want. For example, suppose that you have invested heavily in awareness marketing. This generates a large number of engaged contacts that enjoy the high-level content you are creating. But this may give you no real resolution into the types of products or solutions that they need. To see how this comes about, consider the schema of marketing automation activities in a typical system shown in Table 3.2.

The data in this schema does provide a record of instances in which customers saw content and perhaps interacted with it. But

Table 3.2   Marketing Automation Activities

Column	Description
mktpersonId	Unique ID for the lead
activityDateTime	Time that the activity occurred
Campaign	Name of the campaign
activityType	Type of activity, such as lead created, email opened, etc.

there is not necessarily any information about what type of products were of interest to the lead. That type of information could be collected, for example, by tagging campaigns, but this is often not done, especially when the marketing focus is more on awareness than on product. Table 3.3 shows different types of objectives and some examples of the kinds of data attributes that can be used to make the objective concrete.

Decide on the Process Step and Execution Channel The effectiveness of analytics is enhanced when it can be focused on a specific process step. Consider one of the most important processes for a company—customer acquisition. Figure 3.1 illustrates several representative steps in acquisition process. It is possible to consider the entire process from beginning to end and to build those analytic predictions. The problem with that approach is that you may have a new system for generating proposals, and those are not well received by customers. This limitation in your sales process is now being treated as a constraint for your lead sourcing process, as many viable leads may be rejected because of their similarity to leads that previously fell out of the pipeline at the proposal stage.

Another benefit of focusing on a particular part of a business process is that the statistics are often better. There may be less than a 1 percent close rate from beginning to end for the entire acquisition process. In contrast, the step from nurture to qualify typically has a success rate of 30 percent or more. Models are easier to build when there are more successes and they can be more nuanced in their treatment of the underlying data.

Finally, having models for each step helps to illustrate where the process breaks down. For example, you may find that the customers that are being closed are those with a particular technology platform. This could lead to either improved training for the sales team or a narrower focus only to bring in customers with the right profile. Either way, analyzing the results at each step will help improve the overall effectiveness of the acquisition process.

Table 3.3   Objectives and Possible Data Attributes

Type of Objective	Attribute Class	Relevance for Business Objectives
Expand target market	Firmographics: revenue, industry, employees, locations, credit score	■ Aligns go-to-market model with target's ability to spend ■ High-level overlap with target market
	Intent: topics searched	■ New projects or product categories in research stage
	Marketing engagement: webinar and event attendance, titles of engaged contacts, website visits	■ Engagement at the right levels ■ Engagement at the right depth
Prioritize efforts within target market	Web presence: site technologies, complexity, keywords	■ Proxy for customer's technology sophistication and online orientation ■ Indicators for business model and role in supply chain
	Technology usage: ERP, CRM, marketing, HR, infrastructure products, online services	■ Identify minimum level of business process technology to support a solution ■ Early-adopter orientation
Increase customer engagement	Product usage: type and frequency of usage; breadth of usage in organization	■ Usage of proprietary features and/or content ■ Penetration across organizational departments
	Installed base: products, service contracts, locations	■ Opportunities for customer engagement
	Online channel: browsing history, shopping carts	■ Product interest

Figure 3.1   Steps in the Acquisition Process

An additional dimension in the sales and marketing process is the execution channel. Often there are several similar, parallel processes that run through different channels—partner channels, online channels, inside channels, outside channels, and so forth. While these channels share many of the same structural characteristics, the dynamics within each are often quite different. For example, leads entering the process from a partner referral are often already very well qualified compared to lists of cold contacts. If the channel distinction is not included in the model, then the inferences drawn from this combined population are unlikely to be valuable for either channel.

Consolidate and Align Historic Data

The mechanics of organizing data for analysis can often be complex. Fortunately, a large number of commercial tools are available to manage the extract, transform, and load (ETL) processes required for this step. If you are planning to build models for ongoing production use, you will likely need to leverage those technologies. One-time efforts can often be supported with lower investment, but the iterations can be expensive.

Because you are using historical data to make predictions about the future, there has to be some commonality between prior data and future events. If every event was recorded as a completely unique entity without commonality then there would be no basis for making predictions. The ETL steps are the place to guarantee that the data for modeling conforms to this requirement. The following guidelines will help during the ETL process:

- Restrict to data uniformly available for analytic scope.
- Map to a common granularity for decision-maker identifiers.
- Group categorical information into meaningful sets.

a When trying to build an analytic process, it is tempting to include as much data as possible. If the data collection patterns are inconsistent and the content is patchy, then it can be very difficult to accurately assess the model's performance. Instead, it is better to adopt a conservative stance on data at the beginning and then expand to other categories of data as the robustness of the approach becomes clear. Modern modeling techniques, such as random forest, are able to adjust with some variability in the data terrain, but they are still influenced by choices made during the model-building process, such as null value imputation." ?　*b*

The next factor to consider is the granularity of the data. For example, do you care which contact engages with your content or do you just care whether someone at the account is engaging? Does it matter that your equipment is delivered to a number of locations if there is a centralized buyer? These types of questions affect the way that you should merge the data that is extracted from source systems. Once you have established a level of detail for the decision-makers, you can use it to define the independent events in the analysis.

c Finally, the attributes that are available in the transaction streams are often very specialized. For example, some businesses track several million stock keeping units (SKUs) in order to ship the exact production configurations to their customers. However, those businesses would usually not consider themselves to be in several million markets. The granularity of the purchasing decision determines the number of markets. A general rule for grouping is that you want to have at least twenty positive instances for each category. This applies to categories like industry segments, product groupings, and campaign types.

Build Creative Segments and Audiences Using AI

Analytical models have become widespread in a variety of business processes over the last decade. From their beginnings in consumer fraud detection and credit scores, the applications have proliferated to nearly every business process. There are now a variety of standard libraries, including R, SAS, and scikit-learn, as well as hosted analytical services from Amazon, Microsoft, and Google. The general structure of all of these tools is to work from a set of training data structured as a set of rows where each row includes a single event column and a set of attribute columns. From this data structure, the modeling algorithms create a prediction function that takes as input the same set of predictive attributes and returns a predicted value for the event column. As these algorithms are very general, they can make predictions about nearly any circumstances. However, they all succumb to similar types of issues when the data used has problems, such as bias, sparsity, and noise. Modeling algorithms typically produce better results when these factors are accounted for in the data preparation phase. A typical process starts by cleaning the data, creating features, training and reviewing the model, and then iterating if necessary.

Clean Data   Modeling algorithms perform better when they operate on data with stable statistical distributions. Most business data has a variety of imperfections that degrade model performance. Adjusting the data to improve its statistical properties is often referred to as cleaning the data. Note that this is distinct from the work described above to consolidate data. That step leverages business domain knowledge to make improvements in the data stream. In this step, the goal is to make technical improvements to the data that are designed to improve the resulting models. Some common approaches include: null value imputation and null value indicators, culling noisy or un-predictive values, and removing outliers.

The technical term for a missing data value in an attribute is *null*. In a few cases, there may be a reasonable default value for the attribute just based on the data. Most of the time, though, null is an indication that there should be a value for the attribute, but it isn't currently known. There are a few things to be done in this case. First, add a binary attribute to identify that a column was loaded as null. Then, assign a value to the attribute. This is normally done by either sampling from the set of values or by picking values that have little impact on the outcome. With these approaches, the model can still take advantage of information from the attribute in the remainder of the data set.

A different problem arises with attribute values and attributes that are "noisy" or unpredictive. Consider the case of features generated from time series data. In the process of trying to identify the types of events that might be predictive, several different types of aggregates may be created. For example, one might create both an average quarterly spend metric and a trailing six-month spend. In some cases the differences between the attributes can indicate important shifts in customer behavior. But for most customers, these two variables will be highly correlated. If that is the case, it is often beneficial for modeling to remove one of these correlated variables by using a measure such as conditional mutual information to identify which variables are contributing the most new information to the prediction. In a similar way, attributes with a large number of values can be compressed to a more manageable range by grouping the low frequency attributes together.

Noise can also arise from sparsely populated variables. Here are some heuristics to consider when evaluating an attribute:

- The attribute is largely empty, for example > 90 percent is empty and those values that are populated are randomly distributed without any obvious predictive power.
- There are no value ranges with Lift < 0.9 or Lift > 1. In other words, the attribute doesn't seem to be predictive by itself.

Getting rid of variables that aren't useful in modeling will tend to make the model less noisy and more stable over time and it's therefore always good practice. As long as there is a ranking of variables, some of the bottom, less predictive ones can be dropped.

A final common clean-up technique involves the removal of outlier values. Regression techniques in particular are sensitive to extreme values and typically respond poorly to their presence. In some cases it may be appropriate to remove the values altogether, especially if they represent circumstances that are unlikely to be repeated. In other cases the impact of the outliers can be mitigated by using an appropriate transformation such as a logarithm.

Create Features   Since the modeling algorithms rely on scalar attributes to make predictions, they are not directly sensitive to information encoded in particular values or in time series without further transformations. These transformations are called *features*. As an example of content that may reside in a value, consider an email address. The suffix of the email domain often contains information about the country (for example, xyz@acompany.nz is an email address for New Zealand). This information can be made available to the model by creating a feature (essentially a new column) that just contains the suffix of the email. Without this transformation, all of the email strings in a training set would be considered to be unique values and the algorithms would be unable to make generalizations that could be applied to new data.

The situation for time series data is similar. The learning algorithms are not designed to take in time series data directly. Instead, this data has to be converted into scalar values. For example, it may make sense to consider a windowed-average of spend from a customer as an attribute. For each time period, the total revenue is calculated. This value can then be used as an attribute, because this value can be calculated for another time period and used to predict a value for the event column. Note that the analysis done on time series can be extended to cover almost any conceivable historical sequence. You just need a description of how the data prior to each time period is to be synthesized into a scalar value. In this way, ideas like a "customer journey" consisting of a set of discrete steps taken by a customer can be encoded in a form that is compatible with the learning algorithms.

Train and Review Model   Once the data is collected and organized, choices are made about how to build and test the model. In the most basic approach, the data is divided into a training set and a testing set. To illustrate why this is necessary, let's think about the other extreme. Imagine a model built on the entire data set and then measured by how well it predicts the target variable (revenue, conversions, etc.) for that data set. If the model is overly complicated, say by having half as many free parameters to calibrate as there is data to predict, the model is going to behave incredibly well on the training data set. But it will likely fail dramatically on any data that wasn't used to train it. This is known as over-fitting. If the model performs well on the holdout test set, we are less likely to be worried about over-fitting and more confident in model quality.

All models are statistical in nature and therefore predictions have a certain expected error rate. Error occurs in any metrics used to evaluate model quality, especially those used to measure model performance based on a holdout set. The method described above, with a single holdout set, gives a single measure of model performance. Another method, called cross-validation, divides the data into two separate pieces, a training and a testing set, in a different random way a number of times. Each time this separation is implemented, a new model is built based on the corresponding training data and model metrics are calculated for the corresponding holdout test data set. The result is a distribution for the metric with a minimum and a maximum value. This distribution provides a lot more confidence in measuring model performance. In an extreme case, the training/testing set distribution could correspond to the highest observed value for the model metric, and one would be falsely led to believe that the model was much better than it actually is. Instead, the statistical approach of recalculating model metrics many times gives increased confidence in the metrics of model behavior.

Another approach to model validation is to build the model on the past and test on the future. A simple way to think about this is that, given eighteen months of data, the model is trained on the first fifteen months and tested on the final three months of data. In this way, it should be possible to see how well the model would have behaved in the real world if it had been built three months ago. While this should work in general, it can break down in a number of cases. Let's imagine that a new product was created two years ago and purchases have been steadily declining because the product required very few repeat purchases. If the data is changing over time, the historical information that made it a good model could be becoming less and less predictive in each time period. In that case, if we built a model on months 1 through 12 and tested it in months 13 to 15, we'd expect much better performance than if we built a model on months 1 through 15 and tested it on months 16 through 18. If we hadn't done this, the model built on months 1 through 18 could be launched in the real world and significantly underperform.

In order to assess model stability over time, the first question to ask is whether the model performance is stable over time. If there was enough historical data, one could test the model out of sample performance for a bunch of different time windows and directly see model stability. For example, given thirty-six months of data, one could build the following four models and check for stable performance:

1. Train on months 1 through 24, test on months 25 through 27
2. Train on months 1 through 27, test on months 28 through 30
3. Train on months 1 through 30, test on months 31 through 33
4. Train on months 1 through 33, test on months 34 through 36

If there isn't enough historical data or just not enough data, the preferred method is to ignore the time window and use the multiple resampling method described earlier in this section.

A final approach to investigating model stability over time doesn't look at the model directly but instead looks at the underlying data. One could divide the full data into four time periods. For each time period, quantitative measures would be calculated for the statistical distribution of each predictive variable. While there are lots of ways of doing this in the statistics literature, there are standard well-understood ways available in standard statistics libraries. If the distribution of the variable is sufficiently different in each time period, then it is suspect. If it is possible to build a model with good performance metrics without this variable, it is preferable to exclude it.

Once the model is built, in addition to model performance metrics, a number of approaches can be used to give a metric that ranks the importance or significance of the individual variables. For example, the industry workhorse known as *random forest explicitly* produces various measures of descending variable importance. It is worth looking at these variables and making sure they make business sense. This can be done via the data analysis described in the previous section. If they don't make sense, it may be necessary to either remove the field itself or, as discussed previously, a small number of data rows that behave in an unnatural fashion.

It is important to note that the list of most important variables is not necessarily going to help segment customers. Instead, they are those variables most significant in giving you a good model. For example, in a model for lead scoring, one of the most important variables could be a spam indicator. Its utility might be in identifying which leads are in the bottom 30 percent and effectively remove these leads from consideration because of their high spam score. The spam indicator, while very useful, will not help differentiate among the remaining 70 percent of leads that aren't spam.

Execute Campaigns Against AI-Assisted Segments and Audiences

The goal of most model-building exercises is to have business impact. This can come either through the insights generated by building the model or from operating the model in a decision-making context. The value from the latter is usually many times that of the former. Because of this, assessments of analytic projects should always include the feasibility of using a model to decide among different business actions.

The following are examples of process steps for which actions need to be prioritized:

- Deciding which accounts and contact titles to include in a digital advertising campaign
- Selecting attendees for a high-value event

- Including accounts in the scope of a field sales team
- Determining which leads to call back
- Partitioning outreach efforts between experienced and inexperienced sales teams
- Deploying account relationship managers to cross-sell to the installed base of customers
- Rejecting accounts or contacts from list providers when they are unsuitable
- Modulating the time spent by an outbound sales team to develop an account

In each of these cases, there are many possible configurations. Analytic models are the best way to get the maximal outcome from an investment. Human judgment is not as useful as a model when there are a very large number of small decisions to be made.

While it may seem obvious that models should be leveraged to improve operational performance, there is often institutional resistance and inertia. Here are some common examples of undifferentiated operating models that lead to sub-optimal resource allocation:

- All leads are called back regardless of their quality.
- No leads are selected for direct engagement unless they explicitly ask to be contacted.
- Outbound activities are solely at the sales rep's discretion.
- Every salesperson is expected to sell every product.
- Invitations for events are prioritized by sales rep relationship rather than by account potential.

In some cases there may be good operational or practical reasons for such undifferentiated activities. But there should always be a path forward for the organization to leverage the analytic output. Otherwise, the effort is best spent elsewhere.

Having identified a particular set of decisions that the model should influence, the next important consideration is how to actually influence the decision. Here are three basic routes to implementation:

- List-based recommendations
- Application-based recommendations
- API-based recommendations

List-based recommendations are offline processes whereby the set of analytic outcomes is pre-calculated on a one-time basis. These lists can then be manually fed into different systems and processes. One example of such a process is digital advertising. Lists of target domains can be loaded along with targeting criteria. These platforms then execute the advertising campaign. List-based systems can work well when the operations are relatively infrequent and the actions are centralized. Distributing list-based approaches to a large number of parties who have other responsibilities is usually not workable and results are far less trackable than results for alternatives. One example would be distributing lists of target accounts to regional sales managers on a weekly basis. This solution is simple from a system perspective, but it will generally not support a closed-loop learning process because execution is likely to be sporadic.

Application-based recommendations are delivered through a specific application that decision-makers already use. For example, a standalone tool for researching accounts can provide recommendations as well as account profile information. In cases when there is already good adoption of these systems or where the application is to be an essential part of the decision-making process, these solutions can be successful. When the applications are too far outside the normal course of the business process of those making the decisions, they tend to suffer from poor adoption.

The most flexible approach is to have recommendations delivered through APIs. This enables access through existing systems in the context in which they are needed most, whether on a website or in a CRM system. API-based solutions are the best suited to accommodate other changes that may result in a different recommendation.

Measure Results on Revenue, Opportunity, and Engagement Metrics

The best practice for analytics is to make it a repeated, iterative process much like other process improvement disciplines like Six Sigma or lean manufacturing. The insights gathered from each iteration become the inspiration for the next round of improvements. Without a clear measurement, no improvements will be possible.

It might seem that you could defer the effort to build the reporting capability until further in the process. Experience suggests that this is not true. Just as test-driven development has become a mainstay of software engineering practice, ongoing measurement for analytics is essential. Measurement capability should be in place on day one for an analytics project to be successful. This provides the necessary discipline and commits everyone to the thinking that was in place when the measurement was defined. If ideas can't be realized in the report, it probably means that process capabilities still need to be built. For example, a stakeholder in a commercial business unit may want to see that model performance is good for his or her business unit. However, the idea of the "commercial business unit" may not be well-defined. The segment may only be defined for new prospects in a particular region. It may not work for new accounts that have not been categorized, for accounts in different countries, or for existing customers. These types of gaps can always be fixed, but the fact that they exist means that the performance measurement will not align 100 percent to the perceived needs of the stakeholder. Sorting out differences in definitions early in the process removes ambiguity and imprecision.

For a measurement to effective, it should meet the following criteria:

- **Velocity.** The outcome should be observable in a reasonable period of time.
- **Representativeness.** The predictions need to be made and measured in advance of actions that affect the outcome.
- **Resolution.** The samples need to be of sufficient size to show performance results in the model.

Velocity   When an analytical experiment takes too long to run, the conditions of the business environment may change during that time. Markets change. Budgets are recast. Attention shifts to the next pressing priority. In organizations where there is more institutional respect for analytical-driven outcomes, longer timelines are possible. In places where the analytics capability is developing, it is best to limit projects to those that can be measured in a relatively short timeframe (one quarter or less is ideal). Using this constraint can help spark creative ideas that may be smaller in scope but no less impactful.

Having successfully executed an analytic campaign and measured the results, the next step is to integrate the learning into the next iteration. Here are some questions to consider:

- Where did the model perform better or worse than expected? Were there important circumstances that were not well described by the data or the data used in the model?
- Can the business process be changed to capture additional information or provide intermediate markers of success?
- Given the observed performance, is there a business case to invest in additional information to refine the analytics?

It is important to remember that not all analytic projects will be successful. Some failures are inevitable, but they are likely opportunities to better understand your market, customers, or processes.

Representativeness   It may seem obvious that the goal of measurement is to align the predictions to the outcome, but in practice this can be challenging. Model scores will change with time as new data is added. Systems may not be configured to track the time series of changes. Reporting tools are better suited to multi-dimensional analysis rather than time series analysis. And the operant behavior may not be recorded in a timely manner. All of these things will lead to some compromises in the accuracy of the analysis. Working through those decisions takes some time, but it establishes a firm foundation to talk about the concepts being addressed and points to a way to process improvements that can be leveraged more broadly in the business.

Resolution   Because models are inherently statistical in nature, they have to be assessed on a statistical basis. This means that any measurement of model performance is always subject to some statistical variation. While there are precise tests that can be used to quantify predicted distributions relative to observations (the chi-squared test) and tests to determine when two populations have different means (the Student's t-test), a simple rule of thumb that works when the number of events is larger than ten: For each sample of measurement segment, the error in the result is +/− the square root of the number of positive events. Consider the case shown in Table 3.4.

The error is calculated using the formula described above. Just by looking at the conversion rates, you might conclude that the model is not working because the medium-scoring accounts are higher than the high-scoring accounts. By looking at the error range, it is clear that the model is differentiating between high/medium and low and that the observed differences in conversion rate are within the statistical error range.

Table 3.4   Sample Case

Segment	Total Events	Positive Events	Conversion Rate	Error
High-Scoring Accounts	125	25	20%	+/− 4.0%
Medium-Scoring Accounts	290	64	22%	+/− 2.7%
Low-Scoring Accounts	160	16	10%	+/− 2.5%

Common Pitfalls

With a process as complicated as analytics, many types of errors can arise. Data errors usually arise because the data content or process differs from the expectations of the team. Modeling errors most often emerge from sparse data, poor data collection processes, and improper use of data. Business errors are usually linked to a misunderstanding of how the analytical program can be executed.

Data Errors

Almost all organizations believe that their data is imperfect. If you ask analysts, you will often hear: "Our data is bad" or "Our systems are broken" or "We are in the middle of a large project to clean up our data." Usually their perceptions can't be trusted for the following reasons:

- Analytics is more sensitive to accuracy and repeatability than to precision.
- Data completeness is not necessarily needed for effectiveness.
- There are many ways to frame an analytics problem that all produce business impact.

In other words, when you are trying to leverage predictive capabilities, you can often mine the data you have instead of obsessing about a level of precision in the data that is unobtainable. This is not a luxury that the finance, operations, or support organizations have. For them, the precision of the data is often essential. But for analytics, it is much easier to accommodate imperfections.

What should one worry about with data? The most common problems are insufficiency and causality. *Insufficiency* arises when you are not collecting the data you need. *Causality* is when the data that is collected is not valuable for making predictions because it is contaminated with information from the future.

Data sufficiency issues arise when the right information is available, but it is not retained as a series of changes. Consider the case of a company that tracks the usage of a freemium product. As prospects log into the product, the lead record for the contact may be updated to reflect the usage. The system may even keep track of the last thing the prospect did in the application. Now suppose that you are trying to determine whether a particular campaign was successful in getting leads to try some new features of the product. This campaign will have been run at a certain time and prospects will have responded at some point after that.

Unfortunately, the usage information available on the lead object will not be sufficient to determine whether the campaign had the desired effect because the usage data is continuously updated on the lead record. It will be impossible to correlate the campaign action with the desired usage response. As a general rule, it is important to maintain time series data for all interesting actions to enable predictive analytics.

A second source of insufficiency is when business processes have too much variability at a local level. It is not uncommon for qualification processes to differ substantially from country to country in large organizations. In some countries, all prospect candidates will be loaded into a CRM system for sales execution. In other countries, prospect candidates will be screened by a third party before making their way into CRM. Even though there is data from both countries, the interpretation will be quite different because important aspects of the business process are not captured uniformly.

A third source of insufficiency arises when the captured data elements are too granular. Your systems may record sales at the level of individual product SKUs and customer locations. However, without some mechanism to aggregate customer locations to higher-level buying entities and to bring SKUs up to the level of the purchasing categories that make sense for your customers, the analytics will suffer. Essentially, they lose the forest among the trees. Coherent patterns won't emerge unless some common features are available to group the data in repeatable ways.

Causality seems like the opposite problem from sufficiency. Data suffers from causality problems when the data won't be available to make predictions when they are needed. Consider the case of an industry identifier on an account record. On the face of it, this would seem to be a perfectly valid feature to use in predictions. As long as it is populated when a prediction is being made, it can be employed in a predictive model. However, the industry field may arise in a particular way. For example, the industry field may populate only after a member of the sales qualification team is able to have a discussion with the prospect. In this case, the field should not be used for making predictions about the quality of an account list that is sourced from an external party because that list would not have gone through the qualification process. In this example, the error comes from a human step in the business process. Errors can also arise in automated processes. Information about an account may be filled in after steps that use the predictive model. Such data can't be used without the risk of a causality error.

Modeling Errors

If the model review steps have been done as described above, then the models should be free of most technical errors. What remains are errors that originate from improper data selection and event definition prior to the model build. In other words, the setup of the modeling problem is incorrect. Two of the most common errors are heterogeneous cohorts and sample bias.

Heterogeneous Cohorts   When consolidating the data set, it is important to restrict it to a cohort of possible events that are treated uniformly in the business process where decisions will be made. For example, suppose that there is both an inside sales team and field sales team in an organization. If leads are routed to inside versus outside based on some aspect of the business process, then it doesn't make sense to group all leads into one model. This will produce a heterogeneous cohort. On the other hand, if the inside sales team first qualifies all leads and then sends a fraction of those to the field team, then there is a single cohort of leads and it makes sense to consolidate them for modeling. If there is no similarity on how the decisions are made, then it doesn't make sense to impose a uniform scoring on the events. The results can be models that are far less useful because the predictions don't align to the systematic differences in the process.

Sample Biases   Even if the model data is all drawn from the same cohort, there can still be sample biases that contaminate the data. This can come about from structural effects related to source systems (that is, systems that have not been integrated or are not operational for the same duration). It can also arise in more subtle ways from the business objective. For example, consider the case of a model to predict the likelihood of close when a visitor visits your website. To prepare the data set for this case, you may be inclined to include variables that measure how long it has been since they were on your site. For the population of visitors that close, the duration since visiting provides interesting insight about how long it typically takes for visitors to become customers. The problem comes when considering the group of visitors that do not go on to become customers. For that group, deciding when to measure the time since their last visit introduces a bias into the model. The time has to be chosen in such a way that the resulting distribution aligns with the overall business objective. Otherwise, the model will incorrectly weight variables like duration.

Business Errors

Business errors comprise cases for which important aspects of either existing businesses process or culture are not well understood at the time the program is defined. Cultural misunderstandings lead to rejection of the program recommendations because they are not palatable to important stakeholders. Process misunderstandings lead to recommendations that either can't be executed or don't have impact.

Not Palatable   Many factors can make recommendations unpalatable to an organization. A few examples are listed in Table 3.5, along with the objection encountered. In other contexts,

Table 3.5   Factors Making a Recommendation Objectionable

Program	Expected Action	Objection
Expand lead flow by running introductory campaigns to highly scored accounts	Marketing sends emails to highly scored lists of contacts at organizations not currently tracked in the marketing automation system	Perceived to be antithetical to the brand
Target high-potential contacts with direct touch	Sales cold calls contacts to develop new relationships	No sales experience with a pure prospecting motion
Introduce existing customers to new products with a marketing campaign	Marketing sends warm-up email to customers and then Sales follows up with a call	No institutional history of coordinating marketing and sales campaigns
Cross-sell a strategic product category as part of renewal	Sales calls a subset of high-potential accounts with near-term renewals and positions strategic product	Sales team didn't understand why accounts were selected and was largely unfamiliar with less common products

all of these programs could have been successful, but insufficient groundwork to build the organizational capability prevented their adoption. The following checks can help assess whether a program will clear internal hurdles:

- Has the expected action been syndicated with senior leads (for cultural fit), front-line managers (for alignment with objectives), and execution teams (for feasibility)?
- Is an existing process able to consume the recommendations or support build a new one if one doesn't exist?
- If sales teams are involved, are recommended actions sufficiently well justified to enable adoption?

Not Actionable   For a recommendation to be actionable, there has to be a clear path to a decision that can be executed. Consider the case of a program to identify customers that are likely to churn. Given the list of potential churn customers, then what? Is there a budget to offer them discounts or to provide product support that can help retain them? Are those actions already being taken in all cases? When there is not a different way to execute in the business based on a recommendation, then the recommendations are not actionable.

As another example, suppose there is a goal to prioritize existing customers by wallet potential. Once that is done, then the hard question is what is to be done with that prioritization? If the sales team serves all customers in the same way, then it may have limited utility. However, if differentiated sales teams have distinct skillsets, then a customer scoring can help sort them into the appropriate teams.

Not Impactful   Analytic programs that fail to deliver impact usually fall short in assumptions about how the program will generate value for the organization. Ultimately, program owners will have to make the case to the stakeholders about the program's impact. Here are some guidelines:

- Gain alignment on the expected impact to business metrics from program measurements. For example, what would it be worth to generate ten new opportunities a quarter?
- Make sure that the impact is analyzed relative to the next best alternative. Your organization may have a fabulous partner referral program, but if it is already saturated, then it should not be the basis of comparison for new efforts.
- Size the potential impact for the agreed-on scope. If the focus is too narrow, it will be difficult to deliver meaningful impact.
- Where possible, look for ways to benchmark performance— either against holdout accounts or holdout teams where actions are not taken according to program recommendations.

- Raise issues that impede success early and use senior management support to course correct if necessary. If the senior team is not prepared to act on the program, then they are not ready for an analytics capability.

What About Contacts?

ABM brings marketers one step closer to 1:1 marketing, unlike the previous generation of email marketing technologies, which have led to more undifferentiated spam and declining engagement rates. The promise of ABM is that the outreach from marketing and SDR organizations will be contextual and aware of the specific challenges facing target companies. Contextual conversations will lead to higher engagement and, ultimately, more conversions. Having good account and contact data is critical to having contextual conversations.

The quality of account information has improved by leaps and bounds in the last five years as more and more companies have established a digital presence, making it easy for scrapers to collect public data about them.

Meanwhile, the quality of contact data has been slower to improve for a number of reasons, including (a) industry structure (vendor space is fragmented), (b) diversity of collection methods (there is no silver-bullet method that guarantees quality and quantity), (c) ambiguity on legality of collection methods (for example, scraping LinkedIn or Yelp is illegal, yet some vendors routinely find workarounds), (d) ambiguity on legality of usage and sharing rules (different countries have different definitions of personally identifiable information), and (e) lack of standard metrics by which data coverage and quality are communicated (the standard metrics—accuracy or number of contacts are too broad and not specific to the context of the user).

(continued)

(*continued*)

As ABM goes mainstream, marketers can't afford to use poor-quality contact data anymore. Wrong data leads to undelivered emails, missed opportunities, and eventually friction with the sales team. To ensure that ABM programs are successful, marketers should take four actions:

1. *Characterize the contact source:* Three independent factors matter:

    a. Account Coverage—What is the coverage of my target accounts? How many of my target accounts do we have contacts for?

    b. Role Coverage—What is the coverage of my target roles? Filtered for my buying persona, how many of my target accounts do we have contacts for?

    c. Profile Depth—What is the depth of coverage of each role? For each profile, what do you know beyond email and phone number (their interests, qualifications, past employment history, etc.)?

2. *Understand how the data was gathered:* Every contact source uses one or several of the following data-collection methods:

    a. Exchanging business cards

    b. Scraping social sites (LinkedIn, Yelp, and others)

    c. Calling the company directly

    d. Using an app to passively collect data

    e. Pooling contact data from common customers

    f. Aggregating data from a number of vendors and cleaning it with AI/machine learning/manually

As you would expect, the three metrics—Account Coverage/Role Coverage/Profile Depth—are different for each collection method. For example, calling the company leads to very good results in the enterprise segment but can't scale to mid-market or SMB. Scraping social sites leads to greater profile depth but can be light on account coverage in many industries and geographies.

3. *Validate a random sample:* A number of validation services are available that can call your contact or try to deliver email. If you are running a high-ASP campaign, this is a must-have. The cost of validating contact data is far lower than that of your sales rep trying to prospect into a bad contact.

4. *Diversify your contact providers:* After you have taken steps 1 through 3, you will likely find that there are entire segments of your target market that are lacking on role coverage and profile depth. This is especially important for large companies that tend to have multiple products in different geographies and segments. You will have to use different contact providers to make sure you have the right coverage and depth across your entire target market.

In *The Martian*, Mark Watney (played by Matt Damon) lives on a potato-only diet for a few hundred days. A single contact provider strategy is akin to living on a potato diet—it may be fine for a single-product business focused on a single segment, but it won't scale for an enterprise business targeting multiple segments with different products. Getting account coverage, role coverage, and profile depth right across every target segment is critical to delivering on the promise of ABM.

4

AI as the Intelligence Layer

We talked a lot in the last chapter about data and about what kinds of data and analytics are needed to create models that can improve marketing programs, which will help CMOs get aligned with hard metrics. Now we'll discuss artificial intelligence (AI) and understand what advancements in this technology have made possible for today's data- and tech-savvy marketing organizations. First, let's dive into a quick overview of what exactly AI is, so we're all on the same page.

Jeff Bezos put it most succinctly when he said, "Over the past decades computers have broadly automated tasks that programmers could describe with clear rules and algorithms. Modern machine learning techniques now allow us to do the same for tasks where describing the precise rules is much harder."

AI is in fact the culmination of decades of work by myriad engineers who were trying to endow machines with human-like capabilities. Now with the advanced computing power and exponentially growing amount of data available to companies, computers have outstripped humans in some areas and are making various kinds of work and activities the realm of machines, not man. While some have predicted that this will bring about some sort of doomsday, it is actually creating new ways of doing business and helping companies that are willing to harness the power of AI to create new and exciting efficiencies that humans benefit from.

Defining AI

Rather than defining what AI is in a technical manner, it's easier to talk about what has been done in the AI field and to use those examples to show you what AI can do.

Let's start with the AI platform most people are somewhat familiar with: Watson, the supercomputer launched in the late 1990s. Watson is capable of answering questions posed in natural language; it was developed in IBM's DeepQA project. The computer system was specifically developed to answer questions on the quiz show *Jeopardy!*. In 2011, Watson competed against former winners Brad Rutter and Ken Jennings—and won first place.

IBM built Watson to apply advanced natural language processing, information retrieval, knowledge representation, automated reasoning, and machine learning technologies to open domain question answering. According to IBM, "More than one hundred different techniques are used to analyze natural language, identify sources, find and generate hypotheses, find and score evidence, and merge and rank hypotheses."

This is a great example of when massive amounts of structured data can be fed into an AI system and, in this instance, can be used to identify the correct answer to any given question.

A more recent chapter in the AI story is that of Google's AlphaGo, the computer program created by DeepMind (a Google company) that has now defeated numerous top-ranked players of Go, the centuries-old Chinese board game. Unlike other games, like chess, that computers started winning against humans years ago, Go was considered much more difficult for computers to win because its much larger branching factor makes it prohibitively difficult to use traditional AI methods. According to AlphaGo's David Silver, the

AlphaGo research project was formed around 2014 to test how well a neural network using deep learning can compete at Go. The system's neural networks were initially bootstrapped from human gameplay expertise. AlphaGo was trained to mimic human play by attempting to match the moves of expert players from recorded historical games, using a database of around thirty million moves. Once it had reached a certain degree of proficiency, it was trained further by being set to play large numbers of games against other versions of itself, using reinforcement learning to improve its play.

The players and followers of Go expected that it would take years before AlphaGo would be able to beat champions, but it surprised everyone by beating European champion Fan Hui only a year later, in 2015. It has since beaten champions across the globe, and contenders say that the program no longer hesitates or has some of the early weaknesses that were observed, and it has "improved markedly."

This type of neural network is great for using in situations in which there is an inherent complexity to the data that humans want a machine to analyze and act upon and in situations in which a team doesn't know exactly what they're looking for.

Definitions

Given the hype around AI, it is important to start with some definitions. A very standard definition of artificial intelligence comes from the book by Russell and Norvig called *Artificial Intelligence: A Modern Approach* (3rd edition, 2014, Pearson). The authors define AI as the study of "intelligent agents." An intelligent agent makes decisions based on data or inputs. Moreover, the quality of these decisions gets better with exposure to more data.

In talking about AI, we have to separate goals (What is the agent trying to do?) from methods (How is he or she trying to do it?). See Figure 4.1.

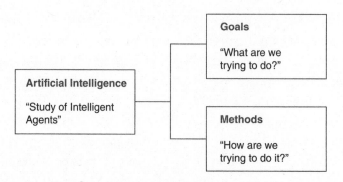

Figure 4.1   Separating Goals from Methods in AI

Goals are real-world objectives. For example, in the case of AlphaGo, the ultimate goal is to win the game, while the proximate goal is to make the best move that would facilitate a victory. Similarly, an AI can be used to classify images, detect malware, recognize speech (Alexa), or drive a car (Waymo) (see Figure 4.2).

In the B2B marketing context, the primary goal of an AI is to predict purchasing behavior, although this idea can be extended to include other predictions, such as ad-click, email open, and so on. Many other use-cases derive from this singular idea of predicting purchase, recommending the image that's most likely to persuade someone to open an email, presenting web content that's most likely to engage a browser, detecting spam in lead-forms, and so on.

Figure 4.2   Goals of AI

Artificial Intelligence Methods—Examples

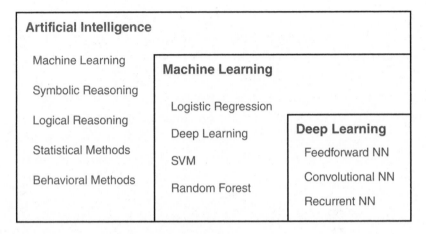

Figure 4.3   Examples of AI Methods

In contrast with goals are the methods used to achieve them. This is the technical terra firma on which these very powerful technologies rest. Broadly speaking, AI methods include a range of approaches such as symbolic reasoning, logical reasoning, statistical methods, and machine learning (see Figure 4.3).

Of these, machine learning has taken the lead as the most promising approach for B2B marketing use-cases. The basic idea of machine learning is that, instead of writing code that uses logical rules to turn data into insight, one writes code that can learn by repeated exposure to data and gets better as more data is provided for learning. In that sense, it mimics how children learn language. By repeatedly pointing to a cat or a dog, the child can learn to call them out very quickly. Machine learning works very similarly.

There are a wide range of machine-learning methods, including logistic regression, SVM, random forest, Bayesian networks, and neural networks. One particular kind of neural network, deep networks, have recently gained a lot of interest from researchers, but we are getting a little ahead.

Let's first step back and discuss how machine learning works.

Machine Learning Methods

Three main AI techniques are best suited to helping companies accelerate their revenue: supervised learning, unsupervised learning, and reinforcement learning. Let's explore those three briefly to understand how they are used.

Supervised learning trains networks using examples for which we already know the correct answer. Imagine we are interested in training a network to recognize pictures from your photo library that has your parents in it—in this instance you would show the photos and train the computer by feeding the correct information back into the network.

In Marketing and Sales, we use supervised learning to create scoring models that tell organizations which customers and prospective leads are most likely to purchase a product. This can be done because the platform shows examples of both successful sales and those that ended in failure. This information is fed back into the network so it can predict whether or not future sales will occur. This information is then converted into a score, which sales and marketing teams can use to determine whether they will pursue that lead or account for an active sales cycle.

Unsupervised learning is for situations in which you have a data set but no labels. Unsupervised learning takes the input set and tries to find patterns in the data, for instance, by organizing them into groups (clustering) or finding outliers (anomaly detection). For example, imagine you are a T-shirt manufacturer, and you have a collection of people's body measurements. With unsupervised learning you can create a clustering algorithm that groups those measurements into a set of clusters so you can decide how big to make your XS, S, M, L, and XL shirts (*AI Playbook* by Frank Chen. http://aiplaybook.a16z.com/docs/guides/dl-learning).

In the marketing world, one way we use this technique is to create segments of customers and prospects, so that teams can create targeted content and sales plays that specifically speak to the types of pain points that those groups or individuals are facing. We provide the platform with all of the data available on a set of customers or prospects and, through unsupervised learning algorithms, the program is able to break the customers into similar groupings or segments that can be executed against by using various marketing and sales tactics.

Finally, we have reinforcement learning, which is also used for situations in which you don't have labeled data sets, but you do have a way to tell whether you are moving closer to your goal, which is a reward function. The classic children's game "hotter or colder" is a good illustration of the concept. Your job is to find a hidden object, and your friends will call out whether you are getting "hotter" (closer to) or "colder" (farther from) the object. The goal of this AI algorithm is to maximize the reward function, and rather than getting a specific "right/wrong" answer with each data point, you'll get a delayed reaction and only a hint of whether you're heading in the right direction.

So where does this play out in the real world, where organizations are trying to accelerate their revenue? One example is at the top of the funnel, where a marketing organization is trying to determine which display ads to show to a lead or account in order to get them to click on the ad. With reinforcement learning, the algorithm can learn which ad to serve to someone to see whether he or she is going to share it or click on it, and the organization can use the information to dynamically adjust future display ads that are shown.

Data, Data, Data

Peter Norvig, head of Google's research arm, famously defended the power of data when he talked about the fact that Google didn't have better algorithms than anyone, but that they had more data, which made the outcomes from their algorithms more accurate. His belief that data is more important than algorithms has created what's generally known in data science circles as the Norvig effect and has pushed AI companies to gather as much data as possible, because more available data will drive better outcomes and predictions.

What are the types of data that matter when you're increasing your revenue? Two types of raw data matter the most: internal and external. It takes both for an AI platform to make accurate predictions.

Internal data comes from a number of different data silos within a company, which provide a complete picture of the kinds of actions that previous customers and prospects have taken. This data can be collected from customer relationship management (CRM) systems, marketing automation platforms (MAP), service and ticketing systems, product usage, or transaction history collected from financial systems.

On the external side, data clouds can collect firmographic information on accounts, including things like how much VC funding a company has taken on, number of employees, and headquarters locations. Other external data can be items like browsing or search history on third-party websites (called intent data) and trigger events in the news that can cause an increase in purchasing probability.

Combining all of this data helps to create a holistic view of the customer; predictive platforms identify the best-fit customers and prospects for a company. Once they have this data, marketing and sales teams can be more efficient with their time and dollars. Now let's talk about some other data considerations that support a predictive AI platform.

Getting the Data Foundations Right

The "data foundation" is the set of investments an organization makes to ensure that the data collected is available for use in operating the business. Predictive use-cases introduce new requirements for the data foundation. In particular, it is important to establish a solid universe of accounts to which all data sources can be matched and a clear picture of when data elements were generated.

As an example, consider a data element like the industry of an account. Many types of predictive models could benefit from this kind of field because business needs tend to correlate somewhat with the demands of particular industries. It is not uncommon for organizations to have their own classification scheme leveraging something like the North American Industry Classification Code (NAICS) or the Standard Industry Classification (SIC) code. A typical process for setting the industry is to have sales qualification teams contact accounts and collect information about the account's industry. They would then enter this information into the CRM system as part of either a lead or account.

Leaving aside any challenges about the consistency of the data arising from the manual processes, the very collection mechanism creates some potential challenges for predictive models. First, the information about the industry is not available at the time the lead or account is created. Thus, any predictive model that is used to score the account at that time will not have the benefit of information that was likely used to train the model in the first place. This missing data can be a significant source of error in the model output. Second, the industry field is not just the industry of the company. It also contains information about whether the qualification team was able to make contact with the prospect. Since the predictive model is unaware of this distinction, it will happily use that information in the way it scores the account. The lesson is that you have to build your data foundation to make sure these types of mistakes don't happen. There are many possibilities, including excluding data elements like industry that are not available when predictions are to be made, adding metadata to the data elements to ensure proper handling during any analytical operations, and capturing data elements that can change as a time series of values so that the state can be understood historically and incorporated correctly into the model training process.

The challenges relating to the account universe are even more complex for most organizations, as their view of accounts is usually spread across different systems. While there is specific work to do to bring data sets together, it is often more important to develop a clear picture of the objective of the account universe. For the sales and marketing objective, the most common operational definition of an account universe is the set of current and potential buying entities. This definition balances the need to be granular enough to operationalize account-level programs for sales and marketing teams with the need to consolidate information from different streams of data (such as contact activity in marketing automation) into an aggregate entity with coherent observable behavior. Some organizations make the mistake of trying to execute at the site level. This leads to a substantial operational overhead, as the very large number of locations leads to a correspondingly large set of changes that have to be maintained. This data cleanup effort often becomes the excuse for not executing because the perception is that the data is not good enough. At the other extreme, there can be too much focus on a global account view that looks across all business units, geographies, and divisions of a large multinational corporation. While these are helpful for high-level executive discussions about overall strategic relationships, these views are not actionable in the context of predictive solutions.

The practical implication of using buying entities is that there has to be a deliberate effort to maintain these entities as part of the CRM system. CRM is the best place to manage the relationships and their aggregation and to assign ownership to the various customer processes. However, even if there is commitment to maintain the right entities in CRM, data collected in the order management system still may differ. Some type of reconciliation will always be required that can link orders to the appropriate account entities in CRM.

For other types of data that is to be integrated, there may not be a clean mapping into the hierarchy that is managed by CRM. In these cases there will need to be matching, aggregation, and possibly duplication of data when it is unclear how to allocate data among different CRM entities. Such processes are inevitably going to introduce additional errors. Fortunately, predictive models can be tuned to be less sensitive to data discrepancies.

Activity and What Matters

One of the many inputs that goes into algorithms for revenue predictions is what kind of activity has been taken by prospects or customers. This goes back to the data we just discussed, and activity data comes from internal sources like CRM or MAP systems. If a lead or contact is downloading content from your website, interacting with emails your sales team is sending, or engaging with your field reps at an event, all of that activity is captured and logged.

If your team wants to increase cross-sell or upsell motions, there is even more activity data available for customers. In addition to the above actions that can be taken, customers can show activity by interacting with training modules or logging into your product's website, and their prior transaction history can also help tell the story of whether they'd be a good sales opportunity.

In traditional lead waterfalls, this activity data was the only thing that many companies collected when trying to ascertain whether or not a customer or prospect was ready to buy. Now we know that by combining this data with a number of other data factors and using predictive AI platforms, organizations can be much more data-driven.

Fit and What Matters

Another data issue to address is whether or not the lead or account is a good fit for the solution being sold. This type of firmographic data can be found from a number of external data sources, and it helps to identify whether or not the firm would be a good prospect. Table 4.1 is an example of the types of fit data that can be put into an AI platform to make proper predictions.

Table 4.1   Sample Data for an AI Platform

Category	Sample Data Elements
Firmographic Profile	■ Industry and Size: primary line of business, range of annual revenue, and employees ■ VC Funding: dollar amount raised by company via VC funding ■ Business Viability: the likelihood the company remains in business in twelve months
Growth Profile	■ Employee Growth: company hiring new employees ■ Investments in Marketing: magnitude of spend on digital marketing and customer acquisition
Technology Profile	■ Security Technologies Installed (McAfee, Splunk, Tenable): which security technologies are behind firewall ■ Analytics Technologies Installed (Tableau, SAS): identifies which BI, big data technologies are behind the firewall
Asset Profile	■ Number of Hardware Units Installed: printers, personal computers, server technologies ■ Laptops Installed Base: E.g. Dell, Asus, IBM, Lenovo, Apple, Toshiba
Website Profile	■ Specific Keywords on the Website: for example, "add to cart," "checkout" ■ Marketing Platforms Leveraged: marketing analytics, social media, lead generation

So why does this information matter so much for revenue acceleration predictions? Because no matter what kind of activity is being undertaken at a company, in the B2B world the company has to be the right size and have the right kind of profile to be a prospective buyer. By ensuring that the company itself is a good fit for your predictive model, other data like activity and intent can be layered on top to see whether the prospect is ready to buy now or if he or she needs to be nurtured a bit longer.

Intent and What Matters

Intent is one of the newer types of data available to teams and, when used the right way, can be incredibly important to predictive algorithms. What is intent data? There are a few different definitions, but at its core, intent data shows businesses which prospects are actively searching for a particular solution, but haven't yet reached out to their company to start a sales cycle. In just a few short years, intent data has become the darling of the B2B marketing world.

Intent data provides an indicator of a company's willingness to engage (Figure 4.4) with you. The stronger the signal, the more likely they are to respond to your outreach. Why is that? Because intent data shows which companies are actively interested in a particular topic or solving a particular problem. It is a time-based signal that, when used with predictive scores for your leads and accounts, will let you figure out *when* the best time is to reach out to the account.

When used properly, intent data is incredibly powerful and has the ability to make marketing and sales more efficient. After dominating the B2C world, it broke into the B2B marketing scene as the silver bullet that many people thought would fix all their demand-gen issues. Making sales and marketing efforts more effective will increase the revenue of any business, and companies were chomping at the bit to understand exactly when a prospect was ready to purchase a particular solution.

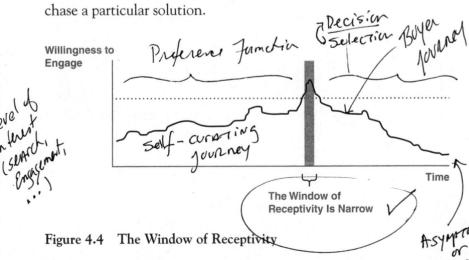

Figure 4.4   The Window of Receptivity

However, intent data isn't a silver bullet. Some people believe raw intent data is like an uncut diamond—it's valuable, but has yet to achieve its true potential. These people believe companies need to understand how to properly transform, analyze, and use intent data to maximize its effectiveness, in the same way that a jeweler polishes and cuts a rough diamond to uncover its hidden beauty. However, others believe that intent data is like pixie dust, something that can just be sprinkled onto another item to magically improve it. Lattice Engines falls into the diamond in the rough camp, but intent data is still a new enough tool in the B2B world that this argument is likely to continue for a few more years.

We are now in the next stage of intent, where B2B companies are becoming more sophisticated in how they use intent data. Among our customer base we've seen strong correlation between the strength of the intent signal and conversion rate. Solution providers are now integrating intent data with other types of data and creating sophisticated predictive models that can show businesses, in real time, which prospects have an active interest in their solutions. Once companies can see this level of detail (Figure 4.5), they can utilize it in a number of marketing and sales programs and start seeing positive correlations between the strength of an intent score, and the conversion rates of their funnel.

Figure 4.5   Two Customers' Intent Data

Intent Data Tells What Content Companies Searched, Engaged with, and Consumed

Let's take a step back: intent data indicates whether or not a prospect is interested and actively looking for a solution to a problem, but how do you find and identify those signals? Intent is aggregated from multiple sources, because it's expressed in multiple ways:

- Online (off-site): searches, forums, blogs, ad clicks, etc.
- Online (on-site): anonymous interactions on brand-owned properties (your own website), etc.
- Offline: third-party event attendance, offline purchases, etc.

[handwritten annotation: ℓ on-site | ² store visit]

When analyzed properly, intent data can show you the prospects that are interested in purchasing your solution right now. However, only when it is combined with other types of data, such as firmographics or technographics, can it show companies a full picture of what is happening at their account and provide true predictive insights.

For example, ten different people from the same company may be searching for a solution your company sells, which shows high intent. However, what if that company happens to be in the education industry, which you may not sell to at all. You'll reach out to the company only to find that it's not in your "sweet spot," having wasted precious marketing and sales resources. That's why it's critical to combine intent with other data, such as firmographics, fit, and technographic (see Figure 4.6), to make sure the prospect looks like your ideal customer and is actively interested in your solution. When all this data is combined, predictive marketing and sales solutions can make an immediate impact on your bottom line by predicting who is most likely to buy, what they're likely to buy, and when.

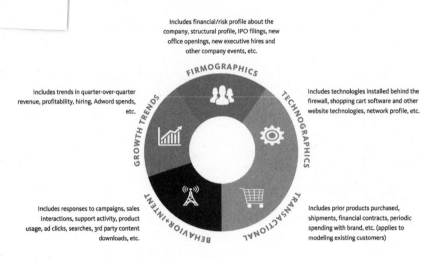

Includes financial/risk profile about the company, structural profile, IPO filings, new office openings, new executive hires and other company events, etc.

Includes trends in quarter-over-quarter revenue, profitability, hiring, Adword spends, etc.

Includes technologies installed behind the firewall, shopping cart software and other website technologies, network profile, etc.

Includes responses to campaigns, sales interactions, support activity, product usage, ad clicks, searches, 3rd party content downloads, etc.

Includes prior products purchased, shipments, financial contracts, periodic spending with brand, etc. (applies to modeling existing customers)

Figure 4.6   Data Categories

Transform Raw Intent Data to Maximize Its Effectiveness

When raw intent data is properly transformed, it provides valuable, deep insights that can help marketing and sales teams focus their efforts on the right accounts and use the right messages. However, you need to understand the transformation you need to create, when and why the intent signals are important, and how to use that information. It's vital to have processes in place, either through your company or through a solution provider, to properly transform intent signals from raw data to predictive insights.

Intent data can be difficult to work with, because it varies in time, and that adds more complexity. In order to properly utilize intent data in modeling, Lattice has created a "topic intent score" that shows the density of companies (that is, how many companies show average amounts of intent for a particular topic). This enables us to see the distribution of the company universe (Figure 4.7) and to identify the companies that actually have high intent for a specific topic, at a given point in time.

In this manner, Lattice is able to classify what companies are showing intent and the level of intent they are showing. We pull in raw intent data, apply the transformation, and then provide that

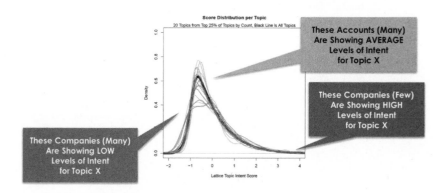

Figure 4.7 Distribution by Intent

information to customers within their MAP or CRM systems, via their integrations with Lattice. Customers can separate companies that have high levels of intent from those with low levels and focus their high-touch efforts, such as sales calls or field events, on those companies showing high levels of intent. For those accounts with low levels of intent, companies can put them into re-nurture and other lower engagement programs, using a chart like the sample in Figure 4.8.

Once intent data has been transformed from raw signals into specific insights, teams can easily see what companies are showing very high levels of intent on particular topics. This knowledge can then be put into action by sales and marketing teams through their

Intent Topics			
Topic A	Topic B	Topic C	...
Company A	Very High	Low	Low	...
Company B	—	—	—	...
Company C	High	Very High	Medium	...
...	...	...	...	...

Figure 4.8 Sample Chart Matching Companies and Intent

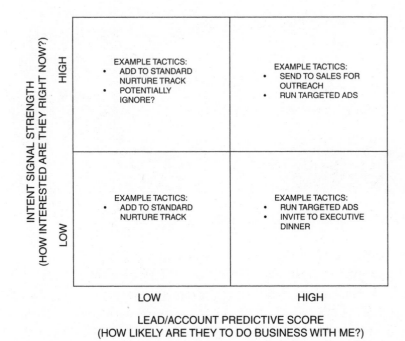

Figure 4.9   Sample Framework to Drive Outbound Tactics

existing workflows. Figure 4.9 provides a sample framework for how you can use a combination of predictive score and intent signals to drive very targeted outbound tactics.

Practical Applications for Intent Data

Intent data has numerous practical applications within predictive marketing and sales activities. It makes campaigns much more specific and effective by allowing teams to drill down to very basic levels of data, identify prospects that are in the market for a solution right now, and tailor content and messaging based on those intent signals. Let's walk through how one of our customers, an enterprise back-up and recovery solution, uses intent data from Lattice to super-charge its account-based marketing activities.

Every two weeks the company pulls in a list from Lattice of companies that are showing high intent in key topic areas such as online backup and data recovery. They then segment the companies

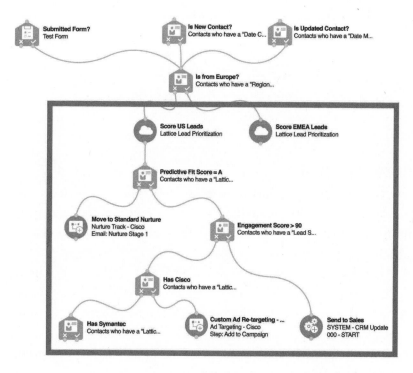

Figure 4.10   Flow Chart for Targeted Advertising Program

based on fit, behavior, company size, and technology attributes. This segmentation dictates which four-touch email nurture stream a prospect is filtered into. As soon as a contact clicks a lead in any of the emails, they are automatically added to a targeted advertising program called Demandbase, through which they receive relevant ads with the same messaging as the emails. The flow chart for the system is shown in Figure 4.10.

On the sales side, once the first email goes out in the nurture campaign, a sales development representative calls key contacts at the account. Using details from the intent signals and other account insights, he or she tailors the call script based on the customer's interests, company size, and technologies that are already deployed. For example, has the company expressed interest in enterprise security? Perhaps the SDR should lead with a message about best-in-class enterprise security capabilities. Possible levels of interest are shown in Figure 4.11.

New Lead	Change Status	Change Owner				A B C D E F G H I J K L M N (	
Action	Name	Company	State/Province	Email	Lattice Fit Score	Lattice Engagement Sco...	
Edit | Del | ⊕	Valencia, Maria	Qualys	New York	mvalencia@qualys...	HIGH	84	
Edit | Del | ⊕	Steele, Jim	BigLife Inc.	Connecticut	info@salesforce.com	MEDIUM	70	
Edit | Del | ⊕	Hawardson, Cindy	Howardson Tech, Inc.		howardson_cindy@..	HIGH	42	
Edit | Del | ⊕	Gardner, John	3C Systems	Massachusetts	john@3csystems.cor	HIGH	250-500	
Edit | Del | ⊕	Smith, Andy	Universal Technolo...	Connecticut	info@salesforce.com	MEDIUM	24	

Figure 4.11   Screen Shot of the Call Screen

With this level of integration, both marketing and sales can serve up the same customized messages and offers to key accounts. They are able to take immediate action on real-time interest from customers and drive increased conversions and improve the velocity of their sales pipeline.

Another great opportunity provided by intent data is the level of granularity it can show. An enterprise security vendor we worked with was able to determine the varying levels of interest and intent its prospects were showing for more than ten different kinds of security topics (Figure 4.12). This enabled them to make the content in their marketing programs very specific and to target the right contacts with the right message.

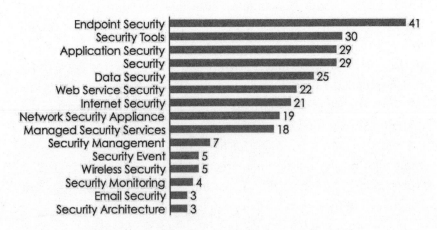

Figure 4.12   Unique Views by Topic Over Six Weeks

Intent Signals Are Infrequent but Incredibly Valuable

While harnessing intent data is extremely beneficial for companies, as we've seen in the earlier examples, intent data is not always available within a given market segment. Why not? Well, employees of companies may use multiple devices to browse and search the web (their mobile devices, their home computers, their work computers) and as a result, companies may not capture all the intent out there. Additionally, third-party intent data is typically anonymous at the individual level for privacy purposes. So while you may know that ten people from GE are interested in enterprise security, it's difficult to discern whether they are from different buying centers or the same buying center (for example, GE Capital or GE Aviation).

Based on research that the Lattice Engines data science team has done, fewer than 2 percent of companies demonstrate *high* intent for a *specific* topic at a given time. See Figure 4.13.

For example, a Fortune 500 global communications provider wanted to include intent data in their predictive marketing and sales models. They looked at a set of 40,000 prospective companies

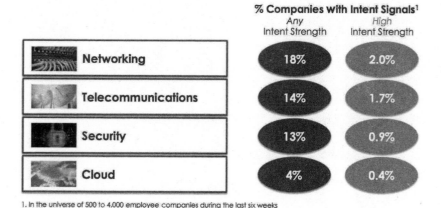

1. In the universe of 500 to 4,000 employee companies during the last six weeks

Figure 4.13   Intent vs. High Intent

to determine what intent signals they were showing. Only 28 percent of companies showed any intent, and only 3 percent of those were showing high intent for any of the four categories that were measured: networking, telecommunications, security, and cloud, seen in Figure 4.14.

It is crucial to add intent data into predictive models along-side other data, although much of the time intent data is not actu-ally available for a given topic. However, when intent signals are there, they can be highly predictive and contribute to increased conversions and revenue for companies. The company whose data is shown in Figure 4.14 is now able to set up high-touch engage-ments for that 3 percent of prospects showing high intent, while those with medium/low intent can be put into nurture campaigns to ensure they have awareness of the company. This way the market-ing and sales teams are able to focus the bulk of their energy, time, and money on the most promising accounts. And the other pros-pect accounts won't be ignored; they will be nurtured with relevant content, so when they are ready to purchase they will be aware of the brand value.

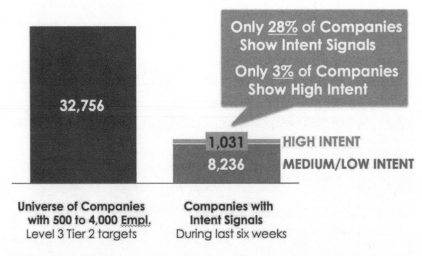

Figure 4.14   Percentage of Companies Showing Intent vs. Those with High Intent

A Final Word on Intent Data

Intent data in predictive modeling gives companies a deep understanding of what their customers are interested in, which can enhance targeted marketing and sales activities.

To maximize their success using intent data, companies need to transform the raw, original object into something more valuable, just like a diamond in the rough. Intent signals are important, but they're not the silver bullet that will fix all of your demand creation problems. Adding intent data to the other data collected on prospects, such as technology attributes, firmographics, and behavior, enables companies to get a 360-degree view of their customers.

This 360-degree view is the real silver bullet. If companies have a clear picture of who their target customers are and when they're in the market, they can make marketing and sales campaigns more contextual and relevant, creating instant improvements in their bottom line. So after all this discussion, do you still believe in pixie dust, or are you going to look for a diamond in the rough?

Clean Data and What Matters

Now that you understand what kind of data to use, many of you may be panicking that your data is not even close to ready for these kinds of applications! We get it. Your data isn't exactly what you'd like it to be. Perhaps your efforts to become more data-driven in your marketing and sales are often frustrated or stymied by data issues. You might be in the midst of a data cleanup effort with IT and new system architectures that seems never-ending. You might be struggling with null values in your data, poor linkages between data sources, such as the links among marketing, sales, and transaction data. The reality is that no organization's data is perfect, nor even as good as many within the organization would like it to be.

The good news, however, is that you can still put the limited data that you do have to good use. In fact, we'd contend that the cost of messy data is far lower than you might think, and certainly far lower than the cost of doing nothing. To illustrate this point, we took the data that we used to build a conversion model for a Fortune 1000 software company and removed half of the successful conversions, effectively simulating the messy and incomplete data that we often see in our customers' databases.

Predictive models still perform well, even with imperfect data While the model quality did decline slightly, Lattice's Predictive Insights Platform was still able to provide significant value, by predicting roughly 60 percent of the conversions in the top 20 percent of the leads. In Figure 4.15, the top line represents the model with perfect data, the middle line represents the model with messy data, and the lower line represents a non-data-driven approach to sales and marketing, with each lead receiving equal treatment.

The cost of imperfect data is far lower than the cost of doing nothing The figure also serves to illustrate another key point: the cost of doing nothing. As you can see, while there is a small

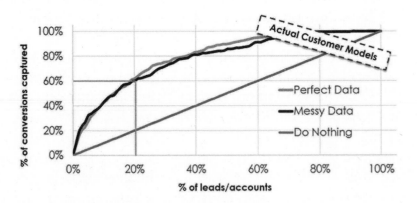

Figure 4.15   Messy Data Still Achieves Results

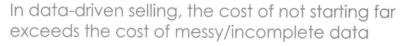

In data-driven selling, the cost of not starting far exceeds the cost of messy/incomplete data

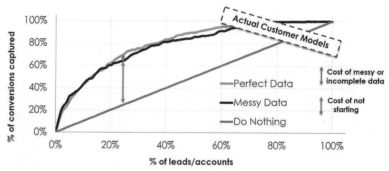

Figure 4.16   Comparing the Costs of Messy Data and Doing Nothing

gap between models with perfect data (top line) and imperfect data (the middle line), there is a much larger gap between an undifferentiated approach (bottom line) and both the top and middle lines. Therefore, as you can see in Figure 4.16, it's a more cost-effective decision to move forward with slightly messy data, rather than wait longer and hope that someday you'll have perfect data to work with.

If we assume the company in Figure 4.16 has $100M/year in revenue and an evenly distributed purchase price, we can quantify this difference by calculating the number of missed conversions at any given point in the curve.

As you can see by the difference in the left bar (do nothing) and the right bar (total) in Figure 4.17, the cost of not starting is higher than the cost of messy data, even if your organization has significant sales capacity. Indeed, the cost of doing nothing, especially for the sake of imperfect data, is in the tens of millions of dollars. At Lattice we are proud of our track record of helping customers capture the value that exists in their data.

Cost of not starting with data-driven selling exceeds cost of messy or incomplete data

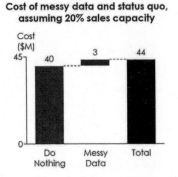

Figure 4.17 Cost of Not Starting

Bringing All of These Things Together

In the world of B2B businesses, the leading AI technologies are the predictive marketing and sales applications. For tasks like targeting accounts, micro-segmenting audiences, and matching optimal actions, they are starting to take over the workloads of marketers and insides-sales professionals. How do you know whether the new AI is right for your business? In our experience with over 250+ deployments, we have learned to look for five signatures:

Is your team faced with a large choice of possible actions on a given day? Companies with large marketing databases or reps covering a large territory will be the first to benefit from new AI.

Are there sufficient examples of success? Success events vary from organization to organization. Ideally, you would use Closed-Won, but there are cases where "conversion to opportunity" or "meeting setup" is more appropriate. We look for at least one hundred examples of past success.

Are you diligent about capturing interactions with prospects and customers? Three kinds of data contribute to picking the winners: (a) Fit (this is all about the company, the firmographics, technographics, credit score, etc.), (b) Intent (this is data about the browsing behavior of your prospects), and (c) Activity/Engagement (this is data about the prospect's interaction with you, as captured in your CRM, MAM, web analytics, transactions, product usage history, etc.).

Is there a wide variance in performance at the rep level? A recent study by the Bridge Group showed that the median rep takes more than two years to ramp up. This results in a three to ten times difference in performance between the top rep and the median rep. Predictive sales can significantly shorten the time to ramp up by giving new reps attractive prospects.

Do marketing and sales aspire to work as a single revenue team? You may not be there yet, but are you at least trying? The greatest impact of predictive marketing and sales is felt in organizations in which everyone is focused on revenue together.

When we first started rolling out our predictive applications in 2010, we found that we could usually outperform more than 50 percent of reps in an organization. Over time that number has crept up to more than 90 percent on average and over 100 percent in some cases. If you are running an inside sales organization or an SDR team, you should find out how well your current team stacks up against a machine that is keeping track of every event across more than 20M companies and learning from every customer that you have ever acquired.

Remember that AI will not replace your reps or marketers. But it will significantly enhance their ability to do the right thing one customer at a time. The AI moment for marketing and sales has already arrived for most organizations, and we can make sure yours is ready for AI. Read on to understand the different use-cases for which teams are using AI to see real revenue success.

5

Use-Cases Unveiled

ONE OF THE biggest hurdles we see marketing teams face is how they actually should be using predictive technology and artificial intelligence to support their account-centric activities. Teams understand they should be doing it, and are ready to dive in, but having a high-level, educational understanding of the solution and actually putting it into action are two different things.

This is an area that we've been focused on for a very long time. We noticed patterns in how our customers were getting value from predictive marketing and sales and the problems they were trying to solve. This led us to create a framework of use-cases that support the various problems that companies can solve with predictive technologies. These are based on the products companies are selling (taking into account average selling price and target market), as well as whether they're executing inbound and/or outbound motions.

We've established four main areas of use-cases (Figure 5.1) where predictive and AI create strong ROI for companies employing account-centric strategies with their marketing and sales programs. These four areas stretch across the entire revenue funnel, and within

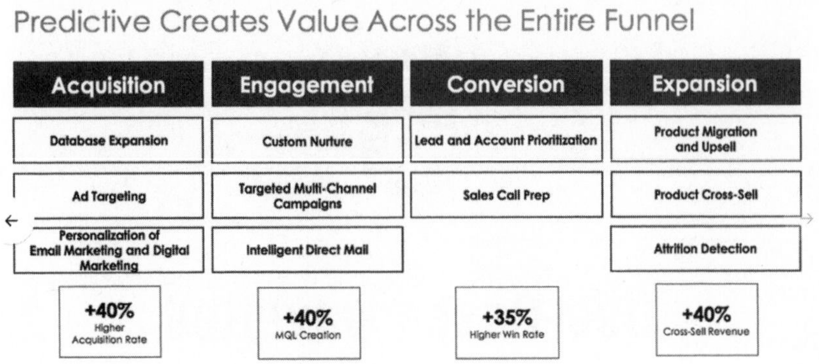

Predictive Creates Value Across the Entire Funnel

Acquisition	Engagement	Conversion	Expansion
Database Expansion	Custom Nurture	Lead and Account Prioritization	Product Migration and Upsell
Ad Targeting	Targeted Multi-Channel Campaigns	Sales Call Prep	Product Cross-Sell
Personalization of Email Marketing and Digital Marketing	Intelligent Direct Mail		Attrition Detection
+40% Higher Acquisition Rate	+40% MQL Creation	+35% Higher Win Rate	+40% Cross-Sell Revenue

Figure 5.1   Value Across the Funnel

each area are specific programs and campaigns that companies should execute against to begin seeing improved efficiencies in their revenue funnel:

Acquisition

- Database Expansion
- Ad Targeting
- Personalized Email and Digital Marketing

Engagement

- Targeted Multi-Channel Campaigns
- Customer Nurture
- Intelligent Direct Mail

Conversion

- Account Prioritization
- Sales Call Prep

Expansion

- Product Migration and Upsell
- Product Cross-Sell
- Attrition Detection

Let's start with the top of the funnel and dive into the use-cases and corresponding programs that companies can execute to acquire new target accounts.

Acquisition

Companies that are focused on acquisition need help filling their funnels with quality accounts to execute their programs against. This can be an issue for companies that are moving into new markets or for companies with rapid growth goals that know they don't have the correct volume of target accounts in their database to meet those company metrics.

In the past, marketing teams might have just tried buying lists of leads, and then filtering those new leads through various campaigns, hoping that some would be high enough quality that they could pass them along to sales. In case it's not clear from that sentence, this is a huge waste of time. Companies would spend astronomical amounts of money on those lists and the programs they ran against them, and often saw that barely 1 percent of leads converted into real pipeline opportunities.

Smart companies today know that the goal should be to bring qualified accounts into their database and, using predictive and AI, create targeted campaigns (Figure 5.2) to run against those new

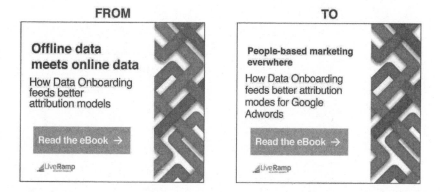

Figure 5.2   Targeted Ads

accounts. With these kinds of targeted programs, some companies are seeing huge increases in pipeline without spending any additional money on their campaigns, by focusing the highest cost programs on the highest propensity leads. Let's dive in.

Database Expansion

Savvy companies want to expand their account universe with only those accounts they know will be a good fit. But without using AI it's hard to ensure that the new accounts you're adding are actually a good fit for the product you're selling. Let's look at how companies can use predictive technologies to fill their database with net new accounts that actually have a high likelihood of purchasing a solution or tool.

The first step is to analyze your company's history of wins and losses to create an ideal customer account profile. Strong predictive technologies use AI to analyze all the data in a customer's database on these wins and losses, and then layer on data-driven insights based on external data sources as well. With this understanding of which attributes make up the ideal customer profile, you now have a predictive model that will identify whether an account is a good fit or not. This will be based on a variety of different measures, including things like the size and location of a company, how fast it's growing, whether or not it has certain technologies it uses behind the firewall, and what kind of financial risk it carries.

In the past, acquiring new accounts for universe expansion was only based on firmographic data, such as whether the company is the right size and in the right industry. Now, with predictive analytics and AI, companies can drill down to a much deeper level of data to understand what really makes up a good account for their business. With this predictive model, companies can have their predictive vendor help them acquire only those new accounts that score high against the various predictive indicators. Some companies will use a numeric score, but we recommend using A, B, C, D ratings, as this gives companies a bucket of accounts that they know are in the highest scoring percentile for them. Then these new accounts can be loaded into marketing and sales databases, and teams can immediately begin running targeted campaigns against them.

Ad Targeting

Once marketing teams have these new accounts in their database, they need to begin warming these accounts and contacts up, so they have some awareness of the company's offerings before Sales starts doing any outreach. That's where programs like predictive ad targeting come into play.

Most marketers are familiar with running broad-based ad campaigns, but often those ads are served to contacts who will never convert into a customer. For B2B marketers who want to focus their ad spend on a narrow segment of accounts, predictive ad targeting can make all the difference in terms of conversion rates and effectiveness.

In order to execute these targeted campaigns, marketers need to create segments of accounts based on which targets they're focusing on. We've seen some customers target only a certain industry, while others are more focused on a particular size company. The amazing part that predictive adds to the mix is that the segments can be hyper-focused.

Say you want to target companies using Box, Dropbox, and Google Drive and tell them how your offering integrates with those content management solutions. Predictive insights engines can help teams create specialized segments that include firmographic and technographic details and load those account segments into your ad exchange. Then different accounts will receive ads with different messaging, based on which of the three content management solutions they're using. This kind of personalized messaging is proven to have two times the engagement rate from targeted prospects, and companies that are using predictive insights to run targeted ad campaigns are acquiring new, engaged leads into their databases at a faster rate than ever before.

Targeted Email and Digital Marketing

Marketers are also using these predictive insights in a number of other types of campaigns to acquire new contacts and move them into the engagement stage of the revenue funnel. The best part is that these predictive insights give teams the ability to scale their account-based activities beyond the top fifty accounts, and create targeted campaigns and content for the top five hundred or five thousand accounts in their universe.

That is because predictive insights can be automated into digital marketing using tokens or segments, depending on the digital channel your team uses. For social media marketing, teams can create segments based on account attributes and target contacts and accounts with specific copy and imagery that is directly relevant to their activities. For email marketing, teams can use tokens in their marketing automation platform to customize the copy in emails for thousands of contacts. This helps marketing teams extend the programs they're already executing against their target accounts, without having to invest in more bandwidth or technology.

After a team has acquired the right accounts and targets in their database, it's time to start increasing their engagement with the brand and products, to further their process down the revenue funnel.

Engagement

One of the most interesting shifts that occurs when teams move toward account-centric programs is the change in metrics. Marketing teams are no longer accountable for finding large numbers of new leads to convert into MQLs. Instead, they need to focus on driving deeper engagement with the right contacts at the target accounts they have agreed on with sales.

This is why it's so important to use predictive analytics to help score and enrich your target account list. We've seen over and over again that those accounts that are scored as an A or a B lead for companies convert at much higher rates, as opposed to those accounts at the bottom of a target account list. A high-growth Silicon Valley unicorn saw just that once they began utilizing Lattice's predictive platform, where their A+ accounts were closing at a nine times rate (Figure 5.3) compared to other scored accounts. However, just because it's an A account doesn't mean it will absolutely close, it just means the company is a good fit. Marketing and Sales still need to work together to engage with, interest, and ultimately close the buying committee at that company.

By increasing the level of engagement through smart marketing tactics, sales teams are then perfectly set up to begin increasing conversion rates because everyone is working together to target the right kinds of accounts. Let's take a look at how predictive analytics and AI are helping create targeted, data-driven marketing campaigns that increase the engagement rates between companies and their targeted prospects.

Closed-Won Lift by Lattice Grade

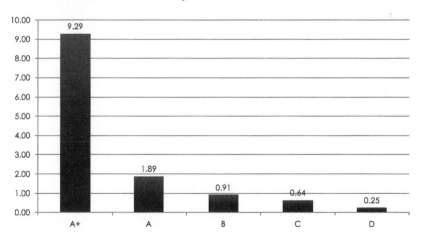

Figure 5.3 Close Rate by Lattice Grade Score

Custom Nurture

Nurture campaigns are a staple of any demand gen marketer's life, whether running a traditional lead waterfall program or a hyper-segmented account-centric program. However, a traditional nurture will have only a certain set of content that prospects move through, regardless of their level of interest or potential purchasing power. And while this kind of traditional nurture program will educate buyers on your market, it will not speak to their explicit pain points, nor explain why your product is such a good fit for them specifically.

With AI and predictive insights, nurtures can become much more targeted, without making a marketing team create individual content. For example, say a company has three main industries they sell into. In addition to creating content for each industry, they can create content that is based on individual company attributes as well (Figure 5.4), such as how much financial risk they carry, how many web-based technologies they use behind the firewall, or what countries they have regional offices in.

Figure 5.4   Sample Content Data Insights Segments

The level of detail that can be easily collected and curated via AI solutions can help marketing teams create incredibly detailed nurture campaigns that speak to specific pain points a prospect has. Through predictive technologies, a demand gen team could identify what the various segments are of their A targets and establish what each of these different messages needs to be about. Then the segments can be fed into their marketing automation system and connected to a very specific email campaign that addresses why your solution will improve multinational companies that carry a medium amount of financial risk, and have more than ten SaaS solutions running in their system. Then, the content that they download off of these custom nurture emails can be industry-specific, so they feel as if your company is personally speaking to them (see Figure 5.5).

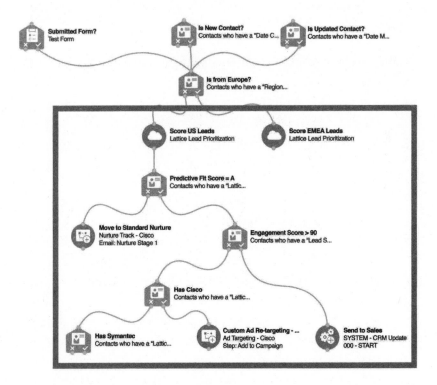

Figure 5.5   AI Email Nurture Pathway

When new contacts are entered into the database, they can be automatically routed into the proper nurture campaign, based on which set of attributes they match. In this manner, marketing teams can continue working with the same amount of content they had before, but tailor their messages to speak directly to their prospects and engage with them at a much deeper level.

Targeted Multi-Channel Campaigns

An even deeper level of engagement is all around executing multi-touch campaigns to multiple contacts within a buying committee at a target account. John Miller of Engagio has spoken extensively about this, highlighting how integrated programs have become and how they need to involve both the sales and marketing teams. A campaign used to be a few emails, but with the advancement of account-centric programs we've moved through the following progression:

- We started with a series of emails
- To a series of touches across channels
- To a series of touches from one individual to multiple people at a target account
- To a series of touches from multiple people at our company to multiple people at a target account

This kind of cohesive, comprehensive program is what true account-centric programs are all about, reaching multiple people within the buying center through a varied number of channels. The goal is always to create a halo effect so people are aware of your product, without being too aggressive and bugging them.

When you have a structure that allows you to target multiple people at an account, savvy teams can then use the enrichments discussed in the custom nurture section to customize content and ensure that your messaging and content are targeted toward the pain points they're trying to solve. They can also use predictive technologies to ensure that Sales and Marketing are giving the same message, working together to engage with multiple people at the account.

That leads me to another important part of multi-touch campaigns—targeting different roles with different messages. A CIO and a data center manager have different day-to-day concerns, and teams need to make sure that the information they provide each contact is customized to those concerns, yet are cohesive so the entire buying committee understands how your solution will solve their problem. Often marketers target the more junior roles at an account, so they can educate a broader number of contacts with targeted messaging, while a sales rep targets the main purchaser with more personalized information and outreach.

Intelligent Direct Mail

Another channel that predictive analytics and AI can dramatically improve is direct mail. While it may seem rather analog in this digital world we live in, with the dramatic increases of email marketing and advertising that everyone receives, a smart direct mail piece will cut through the noise and can make a huge difference in grabbing a target's attention.

However, direct mail programs are expensive, so a broad-based campaign is not a smart use of program dollars; the mailer needs to go only to quality targets. With predictive analytics, teams can use account-scoring models to determine which accounts are the most likely to close. They can then use the insights about these accounts they've curated through their predictive AI platform to ensure the message, the item they're sending, and the call to action are all aligned with the targets' needs.

A high-growth security company executed a program like this against their target market of security professionals, a crowd that in general are adverse to marketing gimmicks. By ensuring that they were receiving customized items that were bound to grab their attention, the team was able to see huge gains in engagement from the direct mail program, much higher than other direct mail campaigns had ever achieved.

This is the benefit that account-centric programs provide teams—when everyone is working together and focusing on the same accounts, it's much easier to move the needle and push people down the sales funnel. And when you add targeted predictive insights, it makes programs that much more effective, so marketing and sales teams become one efficient revenue team, rather than a cost center dragging at the cash flow of a company.

Conversion

Once the buying committee at an account is properly engaged, it's time for Sales to start the process of converting them from an interested prospect into a happy buyer. This isn't to say Marketing stops engaging with the account at this point, but the account is sufficiently warmed up that they need to have active calls and conversations with sales reps and subject matter experts to determine whether your product is in fact a good fit for their company.

The sales team is often the most expensive channel a company has for closing a deal, when you think about the personnel and overhead costs that it takes to run a full sales team of SDRs, field reps, and sales engineers. By using AI and predictive technologies to ensure this cost center is focusing only on the right accounts, who are at the right stage in the buying process, companies can dramatically increase their pipeline and revenue, without increasing the size of their sales team.

Account Prioritization

The first step is to ensure the team is targeting the right accounts at the right time. We mentioned earlier in this chapter that accounts can be scored with predictive technologies and rated A, B, C, or D. This is also true for teams that have multiple models. For example, large enterprises sell many different products in multiple geographies. All accounts should be scored through the different predictive models that a team uses (Figure 5.6), to ensure that the account is not only a high fit, but is also being targeted with the right product!

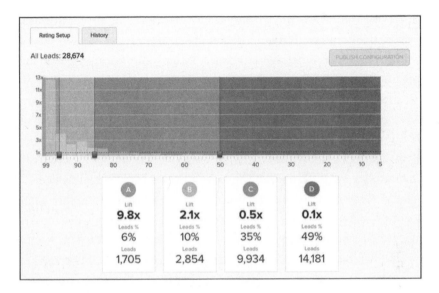

Figure 5.6   Rating Your Prospect Accounts

The most successful teams take these ratings and then prioritize account outreach based on the predictive rating. This means that A accounts are going straight to sales reps, who use insights gleaned from the AI platform about what the account needs. At the same time, Marketing may envelop these accounts with targeted brand awareness nurtures, to ensure that when the sales team does get a customer on the line, the customer is aware of the company.

Then B accounts may be put into high-engagement touches like the direct mail campaigns we mentioned, as they're strong candidates for a sale, but still need some engagement. These accounts may also begin to receive targeted outreach from a sales development team, who will continue the process of warming up various members of the buying committee before passing the account over to an account executive.

Does this mean that C and D leads are ignored? Of course not, but it does mean that they'll receive less targeted outreach, because they have a lower likelihood to purchase any solution. These leads will receive targeted advertising and some custom email campaigns, to ensure that they are at least aware of the company's offerings. This way, if things change and the account starts to show signs of being an A or B lead, they at least have some knowledge of the product.

Account prioritization is a key tactic for smart teams that want to do more with the resources they have. As things often change at accounts as businesses grow and shift, savvy teams will run their list of target accounts through their predictive models on a monthly or quarterly basis. This way they can know when there has been a spike in engagement or a decline in financial risk from a particular account. This way sales and marketing programs are always targeting the best fit accounts.

High-rated accounts have a much higher chance of converting to a sale, but being an A lead doesn't guarantee that an account will convert. It still takes hard work on behalf of the sales team.

Sales Call Prep

One way that predictive technologies are supporting sales teams to close more deals is by providing one place for them to do their call prep, making everyone from an SDR to a veteran field rep much more efficient. Earlier in the chapter, we showed how predictive platforms use AI to curate the right kinds of data about an account, and this data can help a sales rep go from 1 hour of call prep to a mere 10 minutes.

Through the original modeling and customer profile, a predictive platform can show which account attributes are the most important to know about prospects. These attributes should be presented to a sales rep in a clean dashboard, so he or she can go to one spot to learn about the account before making an initial call. Because predictive platforms gather so much data, this must be customized for each company and narrowed down based on what model that particular account scored highest for. So if an account was an A account for your cloud-based offering in North America, the predictive attributes that make it a good fit to buy a particular product can be presented to the sales rep. The best solutions will present this information within the company's CRM system, so it's built into the established workflow of a sale rep, creating even more efficiencies for the sales team. An example of the Lattice predictive attribute screen is shown in Figure 5.7.

Another way AI can support sales reps is by combining predictive data with other data sets. Sales reps at enterprise companies may want not only to see what predictive attributes are key for an account, but to understand past transaction history, or whether other factors can be collected from internal data sets. With AI platforms, this data can be collected and then curated alongside the external predictive factors, giving sales reps one holistic view of an account. Because they have a better understanding of an account, reps are set up to close more deals in less time.

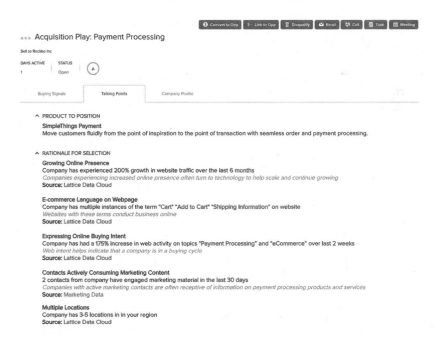

Figure 5.7 Dynamic Talking Points for Sales Reps

Expansion

This takes us to the bottom of the funnel, where teams are ensuring that they expand the lifetime value of a customer through increased cross-sell, upsell, and retention strategies. This is one of the first areas that predictive analytics and AI began to improve when the technologies were first pioneered for marketing and sales use-cases.

Many companies understand their account universe, and find only a finite number of customers to whom they can sell. This is true for those companies that sell to major enterprises or those companies that sell to a particular vertical, like manufacturing. Because these companies can't just expand their account universe when they need to grow, it's critical for them to use predictive insights to understand everything they can about an account to find opportunities for cross-selling and upselling. It's also crucial for these companies to have high retention rates, because it's not as easy for them to replace a customer with a new one as it is for a company that sells to many verticals.

Marketing and sales teams for companies that have a heavy focus on expansion not only need external insights gathered from predictive technologies, but they also rely heavily on internal data. With new predictive AI platforms, this information is all combined together, providing companies with a holistic view of their customers, ensuring that marketing and sales teams can create targeted, customized offers that make their customer base happy, and ensuring the continued revenue stream of the company.

Product Cross-Sell

Let's take a manufacturing distributor as an example for cross-sell. These distributors have hundreds, if not thousands, of products that they sell to manufacturing businesses, and each item has a relatively small margin. Because of this, companies are always looking for something new to sell to their existing customers. For example, if a customer buys tractor parts, he'll probably need the tools to replace them. Seems simple, but when there are thousands of products in their database, it can be hard for a sales rep to identify what their customers might need next.

Enter predictive technologies—companies can utilize AI-based platforms to find any type of data available about what customers have bought in the past and use it to make predictions about what should be purchased by that customer next. This gives marketing and sales teams a direction, so marketers can create a segment of customers who need to buy certain tractor parts and send them targeted emails that show how these parts will complement the items they've already purchased. Marketers can create custom nurture or drip campaigns that provide new and targeted information to the customers.

At the same time, sales reps can use the exact same information to make targeted outbound calls. They can call a customer and offer helpful advice on why select new items can help their business, rather than calling and asking them what else they need. These sales plays are presented to sales reps in their existing CRM dashboards, so they understand who to call first and what to offer. There are other ways to use existing product data in the dashboards as well. For example, a rep can not only see the recommended sales play, but whether a customer's purchasing history looks like the purchasing history of other customers. Or they can see the white space, gaps in what this customer has bought compared to similar customers. Because of these types of platforms, millions of data attributes can be collected and presented side by side, giving sales and marketing teams the ability to know everything they need to know about their customers.

Product Migration and Upsell

Sometimes sellers aren't just trying to cross-sell smaller items, but want to move customers onto new products or expand a product into new lines of business at an existing customer's company. In this instance, sales reps have the same kinds of dashboards we discussed for cross-sell, but the system uses even more external data points to help sales reps understand a possible new line of business.

Often, for these kinds of deals, predictive technologies help identify those prospects that are a good fit for an upselling opportunity, using predictive modeling and scoring. Marketing then warms up the new line of business first by creating customized emails, newsletters, or webinars that educate the new buyer on how this purchase could improve their business. Then sales reps use that same data to prep for sales calls and to begin having smart conversations with the new prospects.

Attrition Detection

The final piece of the expansion phase is all around detecting attrition before it happens. One of the best ways that AI platforms do this is through product usage data and purchasing history. This data is gathered and tracked in easily read dashboards in a company's CRM system, so customer success managers or sales reps can see whether there is a decline in usage or purchases. AI systems can even build in alerts so that when a marker goes below a certain level, teams can be notified and take action months before a renewal is scheduled. This way teams can have a conversation with a customer about what's happening and make changes to rectify any issues before they reach a critical stage where the customer is ready to find a new vendor.

Finding Your Use-Case

One of the greatest things about predictive technologies and AI platforms is that, unlike other types of marketing and sales solutions, when they fix one part of the revenue funnel, they don't have a negative impact on other parts of the business. If a company wants to use predictive analytics to increase the number of accounts in their universe, this doesn't have an adverse effect on any conversion activities they're working on at the same time.

Based on their business, sales models, and type of customer base, every company will find different ways to utilize predictive technologies and AI for their marketing and sales activities. Teams need to start by identifying problems they're having with their revenue funnel. Once those problems have been identified, teams can implement predictive technologies for one use-case at a time and infuse their revenue funnel with data-driven programs. We've found that companies that execute a crawl, walk, run strategy are the most successful. They begin with one part of the funnel and use predictive technologies to improve their processes, then begin seeing improved metrics. They then expand to a new use-case and tackle that. We've seen companies use this process to utilize predictive technologies and AI across their entire sales and marketing funnel to dramatically improve their revenue.

6

Mapping Predictive to Your Business Models

THERE CONTINUES TO be a lot of hype around ABM, and there is a push in the marketing industry for everyone to follow the same new ABM playbook that is being touted by industry pundits and vendors alike. In reality, three things are at play to determine whether or not your team should use a data-driven ABM plan: (1) the size of company you're selling to (small companies have fewer decision-makers), (2) the average selling price (ASP) of the product you're selling, and (3) how long your sales cycle is, since transactional lead-based cycles are quicker, while longer cycles need more nurture and focus from both Sales and Marketing. Each of these requires a very different approach.

Over the past few years, we at Lattice have noticed patterns in how our customers gain value from predictive marketing and sales in the problems they're trying to solve. As our platform advanced and the wave of ABM started to hit our industry, we realized we needed to provide a more formal structure that would help our customers understand what kind of value they would gain from predictive and AI technologies, based on their business models. Our team looked at hundreds of deployments in order to synthesize the different business models we'd supported. We then created a few set tracks for customers to follow and understand what kind of sales motions they were executing on (ABM or lead-based), and we built out the proper predictive use-cases that would help them accelerate revenue. Based on our experience, there are two main axes: What is your ASP? and How lead-rich are you, that is, how large and engaged is your target market?

It was great to see this direction of thinking validated by SiriusDecisions when they launched their Demand Unit Waterfall. The new framework for marketers to use when putting programs and processes in place was directly influenced by a rise of go-to-market strategies based on buyer needs and personas, which is being influenced by the growth of account-centric programs in the marketing realm. In addition, SiriusDecisions analysts Terry Flaherty and Kerry Cunningham believe the rise of predictive analytics and intent monitoring made the shift to this new waterfall a natural evolution, because marketers were already heading toward a more data-driven approach to understanding their buyers.

This aligned with our thinking on the topic in a number of ways:

- It's account first, so instead of tracking leads, the waterfall tracks buyer groups through the funnel, which SiriusDecisions calls a "demand unit." We've seen our customers use this as a best practice already.
- It applies to net new customer acquisition as well as customer growth, which is crucial, because for many enterprise companies growing existing customers is just as, if not more, important than adding new logos.
- The new waterfall emphasizes the importance of using data and analytics or artificial intelligence to better know your customers, which will help drive demand at every stage of the waterfall. For example, the new "active demand" stage uses data to show whether or not an account is expressing intent.

How does this waterfall align with our thinking around business models? Two new sections of the waterfall specifically highlight predictive analytics and artificial intelligence to support companies' revenue tactics. Let's investigate those:

Target Demand   This stage is all about alignment and allows organizations to agree on how many opportunities or demand units are in the market for their solution. The goal is to align marketing, product, and sales on how they're describing their market and how they'll quantify it. Predictive account models can help to quantify who and how many demand units are actually in a company's target account market.

Active Demand   This stage looks at how many demand units in the potential market are in-market by showing evidence of an acute need or buying intention. This is when you want to do outbound movements, because potential customers are ready to engage! Predictive analytics or artificial intelligence solutions can help teams understand which demand units are engaging in activities that signify they are ready to buy now.

As you can see, predictive and AI are critical elements for modern marketing and sales teams looking to better align their processes against their business models. Specifically, companies must understand whether their accounts are companies or buying units within a company or individual people making a purchasing decision. Influencing a group or influencing a single individual to make a purchase takes an entirely different set of marketing tactics. Even companies that have figured out their business model often need a little more detail to understand what types of programs they should be running to support that model.

This chapter addresses the general framework we built to help our customers do just that—based on the products they are selling, including ASP and target market, as well as whether they're executing inbound and/or outbound campaigns. Depending on what box you're in (Figure 6.1), Lattice will categorize your company into a particular solution area—1 through 5—and then recommend the right account-centric or lead-centric programs for your company to follow. This helps teams take the learning from Chapter 5 about which use-cases are possible with predictive and AI, and narrow down which ones they should use to achieve the greatest revenue acceleration.

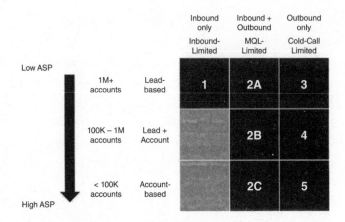

Figure 6.1   Framework for Predictive Solution Areas

Let's get started and look at how predictive ABM and data inputs influence how each of these solution areas generates revenue.

Solution Area 1 (Freemium)

Companies in this area have a few key things in common in their selling cycles. The first is that they're selling low ASP products (typically lower than $10,000), and often they have an ecommerce portal on their website where customers can purchase the product online with just a few clicks. Typically, you'll find that these types of companies have free trials on their websites where customers can test out the solution that's offered.

Companies that fall into this bucket often have a freemium or low-ASP business model through which they actively convert their non-paying individual users into paying for next-level subscriptions, rather than targeting multi-person buying centers. These companies do their best work through a series of inbound programs, and their biggest drivers to conversion are demo requests, free trials, or channel referrals. Because these types of business models have lower ASPs and target individual buyers, they do not benefit from ABM processes and tactics, but they do benefit from predictive insights and AI-driven software platforms.

Figure 6.2   Sample Targeted Marketing Within Dropbox

One example of this is Dropbox converting free users to paying for a Dropbox Business account. This promotion to urge people to upgrade is all done via targeted marketing that occurs within the product (Figure 6.2) as well as other inbound channels. Once a lead has been noted as a marketing qualified lead (MQL), sales teams can do their own outreach to convert the user, without outbound activities or heavy research to qualify them.

How can companies with this business model benefit from predictive? Here are a few ways:

- At the top of the funnel, marketing teams can utilize predictive platforms to score all of the inbound leads they receive via various channels. Through AI and machine learning, a predictive platform will be able to score each lead to determine its likelihood of purchasing, as well as enrich the lead with data on why it's a good fit. These scores can then be used to identify which leads are high-quality MQLs, and which should continue to be nurtured.
- Marketing then turns the high-quality MQLs over to the sales team, which can use the scores to prioritize their efforts and filter out noise from junk leads that clog up the funnel. This makes the sales team's outbound activities much more efficient.
- Sales can also use the enriched data to create targeted outbound communications, ensuring they are having a meaningful conversation with the lead. This shortens the team's prep time,

creates more efficiencies, and enables them to close more deals because they have a 360-degree view of prospective customers.

Teams can follow some best practices to increase their ROI on predictive even further. One big area is creating separate models, especially when there are large numbers of leads coming in. Creating different models for each product line and geographic area ensures that the models can identify the leads that have a high propensity to purchase.

The same goes for creating multiple models for various channels, such as differentiating between channels for hand-raisers (free trial or contact pages) versus those inbound channels where a lead hasn't yet committed to a discussion (attending a webinar or downloading content). Because the activity levels are different, these leads should be scored independently to ensure the greatest accuracy from your predictive platform.

A team can prioritize the hot MQLs over the other noise coming in through inbound channels to help teams increase opportunity creation and average deal size. More importantly, it will improve the win rate of any team, because they are generating more demand by focusing their efforts on only the best-fit leads. Any company with a freemium-based model like we described above can use this predictive workflow and start accelerating revenue in just a few months.

Solution Area 2A (Low ASP)

On the surface, companies in this solution area look similar to those in solution area 1, as they also have an ASP under $10,000 and they sell to an individual rather than a buying group. Companies that fall into this category will also have a large database of leads and myriad inbound programs. However, unlike their peers in solution area 1, these organizations are also doing some outbound programs and are trying to identify leads they are missing, because their target market is more focused/harder to capture leads from. They might need to expand their lead targets by entering the SMB end of their target market and to add leads from those smaller target businesses.

In this solution area companies often have some sources that are vastly superior in driving leads, and they're supplementing their inbound MQL creation with other tactics, such as buying lists or resurrecting lapsed leads that are already in their database. They may have a number of online marketing tactics going at once, such as free trials, content marketing, or affiliate marketing to increase the number of leads entering their funnel. These companies may not only want to score and enrich their existing database, but also score and enrich the lists of leads they're purchasing. They could gain from working with predictive vendors like Lattice to identify net-new SMB accounts their sales teams should be targeting.

One Lattice customer executing programs in this solution area is a financial software firm (Figure 6.3), that provides accounting software to small businesses. While they have plenty of leads coming in, they need help prioritizing which are valuable enough to pursue, and they also want to expand their database of small businesses to target for outbound motions. Using predictive insights, they were able to drop leads into custom nurture tracks to ensure that customers were getting the right marketing materials and sales calls throughout the sales cycle.

Companies in this solution area use predictive solutions and AI in a similar manner to those organizations in solution area 1 for their inbound leads, but there are some additional areas for which predictive supports their outbound motions. Let's take a look:

Inbound

- At the top of the funnel, marketing teams can utilize predictive platforms to score all of the inbound leads they receive via their various channels. Through AI and machine learning, your predictive platform will be able to score each individual lead to determine its likelihood of purchasing, as well as enrich the lead with data on why it's a good fit. These scores can then be used to identify which leads are high-quality MQLs, and which should continue to be nurtured.

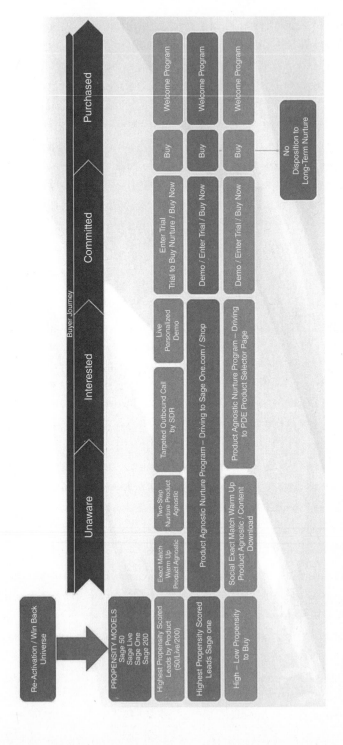

Figure 6.3 Predictive Influenced Marketing Campaign

- Marketing then turns the high-quality MQLs over to the sales team, which can use the scores to prioritize their efforts on these hot leads and filter out noise from junk leads that clog up the funnel. This makes the sales team's outbound activities much more efficient.

- Sales also uses the enriched data their predictive solution provided on the lead to create targeted outbound communications, ensuring they are having a meaningful conversation with the lead. This shortens the prep time of the sales team, creating more efficiencies, while also enabling them to close more deals because they have a 360-degree view of what is important to a prospective customer.

Outbound

- Importing a lead list is an important tactic for companies in this solution area, whether or not they've collected the leads from an event or webinar they hosted or have purchased the list from a third-party vendor. With lists of leads, companies can use predictive means to score and enrich the leads, so that outbound sales efforts go only to those leads that have the highest likelihood of purchase.

- Another area in which AI platforms support these outbound motions is by utilizing intent data to identify which leads and accounts are expressing an interest in buying right then. This information is flagged for Sales so these are the very first they reach out to.

Predictive solutions can support inbound and outbound programs for a company in solution area 2A in a number of other ways. Some of these include improving the effectiveness of events, smarter content syndication and paid search, or increasing the engagement of paid advertising. We'll get into the specifics of some of these use-cases later in the chapter, but the shortened version is that more data and AI algorithms help to make marketing and sales programs more efficient and effective.

So what kind of metrics should companies in solution area 2A be measuring to ensure they're benefiting from their predictive solution? Similar to their compatriots in solution area 1, they're focusing the same amount of hours and budget on a much more targeted set of leads, so teams see an increase in opportunity creation, average deal size, and win rates. Teams in solution area 2A will also see an improvement in call-to-win rates on cold calls, because the lists they're using now are scored and enriched. So rather than going through a list alphabetically or picking leads at random, they're prioritizing the best-fit leads, as well as leads that are actually showing interest in their product.

Finally, there are always best practices to follow to ensure that your company is getting the most ROI out of your predictive solution. Creating multiple models continues to be a big factor here, and teams must not only create different models for various products or inbound channels, but also create a separate model for inbound versus outbound leads. Leads that are on a list versus those that filled out a form may have a similar firmographic profiles, but they will have very different activity levels and intent indicators, so they should be separated for best results.

Solution Area 2B/C (Moderate ASP)

While companies in these two segments have slightly different ASPs and target markets, the types of inbound and outbound programs they'll run using predictive can be very similar, so we'll bundle them together here. Let's quickly talk about the differences between the two types of companies though.

Organizations that fall into solution area 2B typically have an ASP between $10,000 and $100,000, sell into a target market that has between 100,000 and one million prospective accounts, and still has a blend of lead- and account-focused programs. On the other hand, companies that fit into solution area 2C have an ASP of more than $100,000, are selling into a target market that is less

Lattice helps us focus on the "A" leads

☆☆☆☆☆

Updated On August 3, 2017

✉ Matt J.

Figure 6.4   Review of Lattice Engines

than 100,000 prospective accounts, and are purely account-based in their marketing and sales outreach.

A communications technology company that uses Lattice is a great example of the kind of company that fits into the 2B/2C solution area. They utilize Lattice to help them focus on the right kinds of leads by scoring leads at the regional level and enriching their data base with firmographic data, account intent, and technology ownership, which enables their team to target key accounts based on their interest in the various product areas. See the review in Figure 6.4.

Once you get past some of the firmographic differences in these two types of companies, they are more similar than different. Companies in each of these solution areas are selling into a committee and have a blend of inbound and outbound marketing and sales programs running. Certain inbound lead programs work for them, but they typically look for help in supplementing those programs with the quality leads and accounts that predictive platforms can offer in the form of net-new accounts or scoring and enriching purchased lists. In addition to running standard inbound programs like free trials, paid advertising, and content syndication, these companies employ higher touch and higher cost tactics, such as direct mail or in-person road roadshows.

It's within these solution areas that we start to see some interesting predictive ABM use-cases and best practices begin to emerge. Our customers in these solution areas follow these steps to see the best results:

1. *Determine account universe.* As I mentioned earlier in the chapter, it's great to hear that our thinking on this part aligns with SiriusDecisions. Companies need to understand what accounts

are actually in their account universe and Sales and Marketing must agree on that universe before they can establish other program processes and metrics.

2. *Identify and prioritize target accounts.* Once a team has identified those accounts, predictive account models can be used to score and enrich them. This will help your teams understand what good-fit accounts have expressed intent, which inbound accounts are in the target market, and how they should prioritize all accounts for both inbound and outbound tactics.

3. *Get contacts for high-fit accounts.* As ABM goes mainstream, marketers can't afford to use poor quality contact data anymore. Wrong data leads to undelivered emails, missed opportunities, and, eventually, friction with the sales team. Teams need to use a trusted contact vendor, either through their predictive vendor or otherwise, to ensure that the contact data in their system is as up-to-date as possible.

4. *Deliver relevant multi-channel campaigns to targets to drive higher engagement.* Once teams have the account basics in place, the creative part comes into play. Using a predictive model, marketing teams can determine the overall engagement score of a target account. This, combined with the account score and intent signals, can be used to create customized nurture campaigns through email, advertising, and social channels. Using data enrichments, these campaigns can be hyper-targeted to specific pain points that accounts are having or that are relevant to their particular industry vertical. For example, a team can create targeted ads using data enrichments from their predictive vendor. One of our software clients created customized ads based on which demand-side platform a prospect had for their digital advertising needs, and they only showed those ads to target accounts via their Demandbase solution. At the same time, their inside sales team was targeting the same account list with targeted calls and emails. This drove higher engagement with the ads, and ultimately higher MQL creation (Figure 6.5).

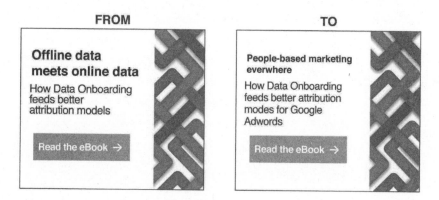

Figure 6.5   Targeted Predictive Ads

5. *Deliver high-quality (engaged) accounts to sales.* Once contacts from an account have started engaging with marketing activities, they'll become qualified to send over to Sales. Teams can use a variety of predictive scores or buckets to determine when an account is ready to be passed over. We recommend that our customers use A, B, C, and D buckets for their scored accounts and leads to help prioritize their marketing and sales activities.

6. *Sales engages with contextualized messages.* Once an account has been scored as an A based on fit, engagement, and intent, the sales team should be taking over, while Marketing continues to support with targeted digital programs. Sales then uses the enriched data their predictive solution provided to create targeted outbound communications, ensuring they are having a contextualized conversation with the lead. This shortens the prep time of the sales team, creating more efficiencies, while also enabling them to close more deals because they have a 360-degree view of what is important to their prospective customer.

7. *Measure performance.* Finally, it's time to measure and ensure that teams are seeing an increase in opportunity creation, average deal size, or deal velocity at target accounts, all of which will ultimately lead to an increase in win-rates at target accounts.

For companies that fall into these solution areas, employing strategic account-centric processes can mean a huge jump in the efficiency and effectiveness of their sales and marketing teams. By aligning these two teams with the same accounts and ensuring they have the same predictive insights and enrichments, companies can accelerate the pipeline to improve the bottom line.

Solution Area 3 (SMB Focus)

This grouping of companies has a number of differences from their brethren in the previous solution areas. Similar to solution areas 1 and 2A, they have a low ASP of $10,000 or less, and their target account universe is in the millions. However, that's where the similarities end. These companies are usually selling into the "s" side of the SMB market, typically companies that have fewer than fifty people. Often these companies are e-commerce businesses or brick-and-mortar stores, and because it's hard for them to do much inbound marketing, since often their prospects are too small to target in that manner, most activities are outbound. These companies tend to have a large capacity for outbound sales calling and typically buy lists for their outreach purposes. For example, a payments processor that sells their software solution to local mom-and-pop stores would fall into this category.

A number of companies have this type of business model. For example, financial services firms that sell into small businesses fit here, as do certain business units within telecommunications companies that target small businesses. Because this business use-case focuses so heavily on outbound activities, there are a number of ways they can utilize a predictive platform to enable their sales teams to prioritize the accounts that are most ready to buy.

One key feature that AI and predictive platforms bring to this use-case is enrichment capabilities. These companies target very defined segments, and enriching leads with firmographics such as the industry, line of business, or financial risk provides a way to personalize and customize their outreach.

Top of the Funnel

In solution area 3, sales reps often want to find new customers and need to expand their target universe, as well as understand which leads are the best fit. They do this in a variety of different ways with an AI platform:

List Deduping Companies in this use-case often purchase lists of contacts for the small businesses they're targeting. However, that information can be outdated or it can be hard to determine which contacts are the most relevant. A payment processor who works with Lattice purchases lists of contacts on a regular basis and wanted a way to ensure he was paying only for quality contacts. They now run any new list they purchase through their Lattice models and only pay their list vendors for leads that score as an A or B. This way they know the leads they're purchasing and targeting are a good fit.

Prioritization Marketing teams can use predictive platforms to score all of the leads they receive via their various channels, as well as those that already exist in their databases. Through AI and machine learning, your predictive platform will be able to score leads to determine their likelihood of purchasing, as well as enrich each lead with data on why it's a good fit. These scores can be used to identify which leads are high-quality MQLs and which should continue to be nurtured.

Customized Digital and Email Campaigns Using a predictive model, marketing teams can determine the overall engagement score of a lead and combine it with enrichment data such as the industry and intent to purchase. Using that information, marketing teams can create customized nurture campaigns through email, advertising, and social channels. Using data enrichments, these campaigns can be hyper-targeted to speak to specific pain points that accounts have or that are relevant to their particular industry vertical.

Bottom of the Funnel

While these companies are generally selling products with smaller ASPs, that doesn't mean they don't want to increase the lifetime value of their customers. This can be done through a few kinds of plays:

Contextualized Sales Conversations Sales also uses the enriched data their predictive solution provided to create targeted outbound communications, ensuring they are having a meaningful conversation with the lead. This shortens the prep time for the sales team, creates efficiencies, and enables them to close more deals because they have a 360-degree view of what is important to the prospective customer.

Cross-Sell/Upsell Predictive algorithms can show when a company has bought one product but not another complementary product. For example, a lab equipment distribution company can see that one customer regularly purchases beakers from them, but no safety equipment. In this instance, a sales rep can find this information immediately, along with enriched data about what kinds of OSHA violations have occurred. This provides the rep with deep context and enables him or her to start a conversation encouraging the customer to buy safety equipment from them, rather than from another vendor.

For vendors that are selling into small businesses, it's critical that they find ways to identify new targets and prioritize the outreach of their expansive sales teams. However, AI platforms can ensure that they aren't just a team of order takers; that they're focused on selling the right items to the right customers, with the right messages.

Solution Area 4 (Large Number of Products)

Companies that fall into this solution area have a defined target market, between 100,000 and one million possible accounts, and are almost solely dependent on outbound motions due to the kinds of solutions or products they offer. Because of this, many of these companies are focused on cross-sell and upsell motions in order to expand their footprint with existing customers, rather than having a heavier focus on acquiring new logos.

Many people who are first introduced to ABM think of it only for acquiring net new accounts, when a true account-focused program should go from net new all the way through existing customer-retention programs. Predictive analytics and AI programs are uniquely positioned to support these kinds of broad-based account-focused programs by enriching data and providing data-driven insights, so companies are able to execute account-focused tactics across the entire revenue funnel. Companies that fit into this solution area typically have a core set of predictive motions that help them optimize their marketing and sales activities and directly increase revenue from their existing customer base.

In order to execute these kinds of activities, companies use a predictive platform like Lattice to create models of their existing customer base by combining external data sources, but more importantly, internal data from a number of different systems. Companies in this solution area often have data on transaction history, ERP systems, product usage data, and financial spend of certain product lines. All of this information is then combined with the information that lives in CRM and MAP systems. From there, what customers have purchased in the past is known, and predictive algorithms can identify numerous activities to support a sales team with these customers. Sales teams should push their data directly into their CRM system to shorten call prep times and provide direction for outbound motions. Some of these different predictive-driven activities include:

Cross-Sell and Upsell

A number of different predictive plays can help maximize cross-sell activities for companies when a customer has already purchased some products or solutions, but there are many other types of purchases that they could or should be making:

Mix Play   Predictive algorithms can show when a company has bought one product but not another complementary product. For example, a manufacturing company can see that one customer regularly purchases nails from them, but not hammers. In this instance a sales rep can learn that information immediately and use it to start a conversation to encourage that company to buy hammers from them, rather than another vendor.

White Space/Category Expansion   This compares one customer with other similar customers in your database. Sales reps can look at a dashboard from their predictive vendor and see that a particular customer has only purchased routers from them, while all of the other similar customers are also purchasing switches and cables. By identifying this "white space" in the customer's purchasing history, sales reps are alerted to the opportunity for a new sale.

Retention

Some companies have such large customer databases that there are entire teams focused on ensuring that customers just maintain their relationships and purchasing levels with them.

Renewals   Companies utilize predictive platforms to look for companies with ongoing subscriptions and warranties and monitor them to ensure they are not at risk for attrition. A tax and accounting software company did this by identifying the super users at each account, based on product usage, and created advocates out of them. When it came time for renewals, they had someone on the customer side who was dedicated to retaining their solutions.

Declining Spend   Companies that sell consumable goods, such as office supplies, generally see their customers repeat purchases on a regular schedule, such as buying new boxes of pens at the beginning of every month. When this spend starts to decline, an AI platform can identify that change and alert the proper reps. This way a discussion can be had about why the spend is declining, and the customer may be retained.

Product Usage   Another way that companies are able to track customers' engagement and identify possible churn before it happens is through product usage. Some of our customers track product usage, an indicator that can be input into their AI platforms. Alerts can be set up to notify a customer success rep if regular usage drops by a certain percentage. Then the rep can have an early conversation about why usage is dropping and identify a solution prior to the customer's' renewal date.

For companies that fall in this solution area, the key is increasing customer lifetime value. Often these companies have a multitude of products and need specific plays created for sales reps so they can identify the best way to increase the spend of their existing customers and maintain relationships.

Solution Area 5 (High ASP)

For this final solution area, we continue seeing a very strong account-centric focus for the ideal business use-cases. Companies that fit into this area have a high ASP, and their target account universe is fewer than 100,000 companies. This means they have to be incredibly targeted with all of their marketing and sales programs; generally outbound tactics are going to be the most successful for these companies, which run cohesively alongside digital activities.

Because of the nature of their business, these companies need to focus the most on ABM tactics. We believe this is a critical component for them, as they're selling a high ASP product into a large buying center. They need to fully envelop all members of the buying committee with comprehensive messaging, through multiple channels, over an extended period of time. To successfully execute an ABM program like this, an AI platform is critical. These kinds of programs require extensive data enrichments, segmentation, and orchestration.

We believe so heavily in the importance of this kind of program that we wrote a guidebook on how to create and accelerate true ABM programs (Figure 6.6) with AI. Following are eight key tactics that we think are the most important for these kinds of programs and how to execute them with Lattice's predictive platform.

Figure 6.6   Plays to Accelerate ABM Programs

Target Account Universe Expansion

- *What it is:* Lattice can help customers expand their target account universe in three simple steps:
  1. Provide the account universe—this is exported from their CRM.
  2. Identify segmentation criteria—examine the region, state, country, international presence, employee range, industry, and more.
  3. Lattice sources selected variables that make up an account universe and provides a master file of these accounts, which marketing and sales teams can start executing against immediately.
- *Why you need it:* This lets teams know they're focused on all of the accounts they should be targeting, instead of only a subset. For growing teams, it's critical to have the right number of accounts for sales and marketing to execute against.

Account Selection and Prioritization

- *What it is:* Account selection and prioritization come down to the WHO. Companies use predictive to identify a series of attributes that determine what type of account is most likely to buy. Examples of attributes include financial data, the type of technologies a company uses behind the firewall, website activity, and more.

- *Why you need it:* The key is to prioritize these target accounts and treat them differently based on who they are and how likely they are to purchase! Lattice fast-tracks this selection by using predictive algorithms to unearth the appropriate predictive attributes for your target accounts.

Complementary Solution Campaigns

- *What it is:* Customers run this campaign by using Lattice's Data Cloud Explorer to identify which target accounts are using technologies or solutions that are complementary to their company's offerings. They create segments based on this data and then determine which products should be offered to different prospects.

- *Why you need it:* Users can then laser focus on targets and add an extra data layer that helps create customized content, which speaks to how their product works in conjunction with those already in use. Customers are able to use Lattice's automated integrations with marketing automation systems to send targeted messages to specific segments.

Competitive Take-Out Campaign

- *What it is:* Users execute a competitive take-out campaign by using Lattice's Data Cloud Explorer to identify which target accounts are using technologies that are competitive to their company. They create segments based on these competitive technologies and then determine which product should be offered to those different merchants.

- *Why you need it:* Customers create customized content that speaks to how a product works better than the competitive solutions to encourage prospects to consider their solution instead. Lattice's automated integrations are used with marketing automation systems to send targeted messaging to specific segments.

Intent-Driven Direct Mail

- *What it is:* Buyers accelerate awareness with identified target account champions. They use Lattice's predictive platform to create two models—model 1 scores target accounts and model 2 scores the leads within those accounts to see whether they're showing any intent. This helps to identify the ideal buyer who is actively searching for a particular solution.
- *Why you need it:* Direct mail is costly and time-consuming, so teams should only use it for companies that are ready to buy now. Once marketers know the details, it's easy to create an engaging mailer that includes targeted predictive insights from Lattice's Data Cloud Explorer.

Account-Engagement Sales Triggers

- *What it is:* Lattice helps condense individual lead triggers into one master account sales trigger. This helps teams make sure key buyers are not discarded as leads, that is, below the MQL threshold and are placed into the right master account bucket.
- *Why you need it:* Individual contacts at an account may not trigger sales thresholds, but if three contacts from one target account are all engaging with your content, it's time for Sales to engage. With Lattice's predictive platform, these triggers are automated, so Sales never misses a chance to reach out to a warm contact.

Events for Low Engagement Accounts

- *What it is:* Lattice can engage high-propensity target accounts that have no previous engagement record through a series of personalized programs. This can be done through events such as roadshows, where there is a one-to-one experience with the highest value target accounts.

- *Why you need it:* Events are an expensive marketing channel, so to get the highest ROI it's critical to invite only those customers with the highest chance of closing. Predictive scoring can help teams determine who is the best fit for certain events based on engagement, firmographics, and other data attributes.

Cross-Sell Campaigns

- *What it is:* Customers can expand the lifetime value of their customers with our insights platform. They use Lattice to create different models to determine where the cross-sell opportunities exist within their customer database, based on what other customer deployments look like and external data attributes.

- *Why you need it:* With Lattice, teams have a dashboard of customized sales plays showing which customers are the best fit for a cross-sell campaign, eliminating the guesswork about which customers a team should target. Then companies can customize campaigns that enable Sales and Marketing to target these customers.

Customers that run these kinds of campaigns see incredible success in targeting the correct accounts with an omni-channel campaign that drives positive revenue numbers.

Bringing It All Together

As you can see, to run successful ABM programs requires incredible amounts of data enrichment and an impressive amount of segmentation and orchestration. AI platforms make ABM programs like these possible because they provide one comprehensive view of a customer's profile, which can then be segmented and integrated into activation platforms like marketing automation, CRM, or ad networks.

Before diving into an ABM program, companies should evaluate what kind of solution area they fall into and determine the best use-cases for ABM within their organizations. That way they're not just trying out some ABM tactics, but are strategically integrating these programs into their marketing and sales activities to increase revenue.

7

Ten Steps to Successfully Accelerate Revenue with Predictive and AI

Now that you have a background in AI and an understanding of the types of use-cases that can be solved by applying predictive analytics to account-centric campaigns, it's time for a rundown on how to implement an AI program to accelerate your revenue. Our team has almost a decade of experience in helping customers get predictive and AI programs up and running, so we've honed in on the best practices that will enable your team to get the most value immediately. Following this framework will not only help your team achieve quick wins, but it will help identify the missteps some teams take that can detract from revenue growth. This chapter will provide an in-depth overview of how to implement an AI program successfully and use the predictive insights it provides to drive increased revenue results within quickly and reliably. We will walk through ten steps to show you how to pick a use-case, get your data ready, train your team, launch, and then iterate. Let's get started.

1. Get Buy-In from All Stakeholders

In any size company, the deployment of an AI platform will involve multiple stakeholders. When you're working to overhaul the way a company addresses the revenue engine dramatically, you have to ensure that all teams are on the same page before any changes are implemented or technology is deployed.

In order to realize the full value of AI, your company must fully buy into the concept of predictive marketing and selling. Successful companies understand the importance of early buy-in, ideally before a purchase is even made, because without buy-in there is a risk that a predictive solution will be perceived as another burdensome tool pushed on the sales or marketing team. Best-in-class organizations use holistic, cascading communication to all relevant team members to drive broader buy-in. Their goal is to make sure that all parts of the organization are committed to program success, and have bought in on the process that will get them there. Companies should be prepared for multiple rounds of conversations about why and how this will be implemented and budget enough time for this dialogue, as achieving commitment may take multiple discussions with different teams in the company.

A number of different teams need to be involved in a successful AI implementation. These include:

Sales Having front-line sales staff and management in these conversations will bring out the workflow-related nuances that can mean life or death for new revenue initiatives. It is also important to ensure the sales team is excited about and wants to focus on the goals set forth using AI—whether that is prioritization of inbound leads, target accounts, or existing customers. Without the input of the sales team, Marketing may go through the entire process of re-architecting how they assess leads or accounts and pass them over to Sales, only to have the sales team treat them the exact same way they would have before the AI implementation. We have seen instances of this happening, and inevitably it increases the distance between the two teams, instead of aligning them better, as predictive programs have the power to do.

Marketing We often see that the marketing team is the initial purchaser of an AI platform, because they recognize the power of focusing their campaigns at both the top and bottom of the funnel on only the right accounts, to be more efficient with their spend. Marketing teams are often the ones who create the ideal customer profiles, based on the models that their predictive platform provides. Since Marketing will then create the content that aligns with campaigns, as well as create targeted messages for various segments of your target account universe, it's critical that their team be fully committed to changing processes in a way that incorporates the insights an AI platform can provide.

IT Building targeted AI-driven campaigns often depends on internal data. Your IT team will need to know which data is most important and pull those internal data sources into your AI platform. Moreover, IT ensures that all internal data is accurate and that your AI platform is following any required security parameters. When we helped a major Fortune 100 Telecom company deploy their AI platform, there were a number of specific guidelines around what internal data could be used in their models and which data was not allowed to be used because of compliance issues they have to follow in a regulated industry. If the demand generation team that initially purchased Lattice hadn't involved the IT team from the beginning, the project would have been dead in the water before they'd even signed the contract.

CRM Predictive platforms sync very tightly with CRM systems at any company, and the CRM specialists will know what needs to be done to optimize your CRM workflow to include new processes and information driven by your AI products. Without their input you may not be connecting the right fields, which means Sales and Marketing will be putting inaccurate data into the models, rendering them useless. In addition, the CRM team must ensure that the data flowing back into the system is properly integrating into the daily workflow of the sales reps. Without that, sales teams will not benefit from the insights their AI platform provides about targeted accounts and high-scoring leads.

A good project manager   Let's face it, these teams don't usually work together on a regular basis and may not even be located in the same office building or state. The success of the project relies on having an individual who is able to manage cross-functional work teams and keep everything on track. It's critical that one person manages the input of all relevant teams and keeps all stakeholders aware of critical decision timelines or updates. This person's role may diminish a bit once the program is up and running, but for the first few months it's critical that he or she keep all channels of communication open between the teams. This is especially important in the beginning, when buy-in may be lacking. One way we've seen project managers increase buy-in as the program grows is to broadcast wins to all relevant teams, using a mix of communication channels (for example, company and team meetings, enterprise portals, and communication platforms). We've seen a sales team leader who was the project manager use Salesforce Chatter to publish updates from its predictive program on a weekly basis, so everyone has access to the information. See Figure 7.1.

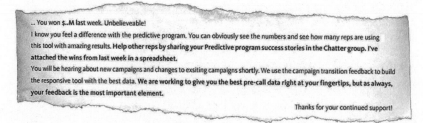

... You won $..M last week. Unbelievable!

I know you feel a difference with the predictive program. You can obviously see the numbers and see how many reps are using this tool with amazing results. Help other reps by sharing your Predictive program success stories in the Chatter group. I've attached the wins from last week in a spreadsheet.

You will be hearing about new campaigns and changes to exiting campaigns shortly. We use the campaign transition feedback to build the responsive tool with the best data. We are working to give you the best pre-call data right at your fingertips, but as always, your feedback is the most important element.

Thanks for your continued support!

Figure 7.1   Sample Chatter Communication

2. Start with One Use-Case

One of the great things about a predictive marketing analytics platform is that it can improve all parts of the revenue funnel. Because of that capability, it's easy for teams to be tempted to try to fix all their identified problems right away. However, companies that go with this approach generally don't have the bandwidth to tackle all the issues at once and end up not committing enough resources, which means none of their problems are fully resolved. This kills any positive momentum that an AI platform provides, and it often slides into obscurity as teams go back to doing things the way they used to.

The companies that see the most success with AI and predictive are those that choose one use-case to start with and completely work through it, putting technology, processes, and people in place to support that use-case successfully. Once that first use-case is performing and providing intrinsic value to the revenue pipeline, companies can expand into other use-cases and find success with them.

How do you choose the best use-case to begin with? Objectively assess your sales pipeline and identify an area that you know has issues. Do your SDRs have too many leads? Then you should focus on a prioritization use-case. Do you need help identifying which target accounts your marketing and sales team will target? Then an ABM use-case is where your team should begin. Or if your sales reps need help identifying plays to grow customer lifetime value, your first use-case should be around cross-sell and upsell plays.

For example, when a high-growth Silicon Valley unicorn deployed Lattice, they wanted to apply predictive to five use-cases—prioritizing existing leads, improving their ABM program, putting structure around cross-selling initiatives, increasing conversion rates, and increasing overall growth at the company. To make sure they were successful, the demand-gen team that was leading the effort worked with Lattice to break it into phases to ensure that at each stage of the process they were addressing all the issues and maintaining a high standard of predictive quality. Phase 1 of their program was prioritizing the leads in their database to ensure their

Closed-Won Lift by Lattice Grade

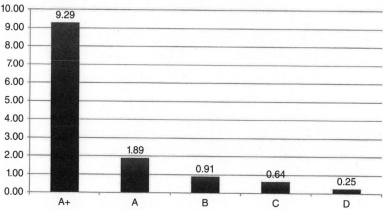

Figure 7.2   **Customer Lead Prioritization Results**

sales reps were reaching out to the highest quality leads. This ensured that Marketing was passing over highly scored MQLs to Sales, while the other leads were going through various nurture programs. As you can see from Figure 7.2, the team saw huge success once their team started focusing their efforts on the right leads in their database.

After they had successfully deployed their prioritization models in place and were consistently performing at the levels seen in Figure 7.2, the team started focusing on other priorities such as creating a client model and creating a targeted account universe for outbound activities.

Your predictive vendor should be able to help you decide which areas are going to be the most valuable to your organization in the short term and help you create your own phased approach to rolling out your AI program.

3. Define Success Measurements Clearly with a Real Operational Report

One of the most important success-factors for any new technology deployment is a clear definition of success metrics and buy-in from the entire team on those metrics. Some companies even deploy a new solution and then just look at revenue in the next quarter as an indicator for whether or not the new tool performed and accelerated revenue. However, there is so much more that could be affecting business—perhaps without this technology, revenue might have gone down? Or maybe the sales-cycles are too long for the technology to show any measurable impact in a quarter. That is why it is important to isolate the effects of a new AI platform and have agreement across all teams about what they'll be measuring, how they'll measure, and the timeline for success.

Two success items must be defined—the first is ensuring that the model is performing the way it's supposed to, and the second is looking at which KPIs will be measured. Model performance is the first measurement, and then teams can define KPIs.

One of the best ways to do both of these is to incorporate A/B testing into your pilot or first use-case, as shown in the model in Figure 7.3. Have one group utilize predictive insights and have a second control group that doesn't. Review the results after a predetermined time, ideally one sales cycle, and see whether the A leads or accounts are closing at higher rates than D leads and accounts. If this is the case, you'll know for sure that your model is performing correctly, and then teams can begin measuring how much of an impact their predictive program is having on the business.

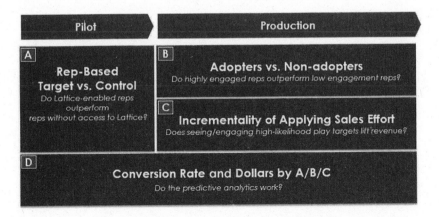

Figure 7.3   A/B Testing Model for Pilot and Production Programs

300%	35%	15%	15%	200%	20%	10X
Higher Conversions	Higher Deal Size	Increased Deal Velocity	Greater Sales Attainment	Higher Cross-Sell Rates	Higher Retention	Higher Revenue

Figure 7.4   Predictive Programs Impact Numerous Revenue Metrics

Teams with an extended sales cycle, such as those close to a year, should look at leading indicators first, such as conversions from MQLs to opportunities or engagement at the account level aggregated across all buyers and influencers. This way any tweaks that need to be made to models, data, or processes can be done before a new sales cycle begins. Teams with a shorter sales cycle can measure things like closed pipeline and sales cycle velocity. We've seen customers measure a variety of different metrics, all based on what matters most to the business. Figure 7.4 shows a few of the different positive impacts that our customers have been able to measure after deploying predictive analytics in their systems.

When measuring final results of predictive programs, there are typically two key dimensions to consider:

- Reviewing performance of individual campaigns
- Measuring incremental program lift and calculating overall program ROI

Best-in-class organizations work with metrics from both dimensions and perform quarterly analysis of performance indicators such as engagement of sales reps with predictive recommendations, conversion of predictive recommendations into leads or opportunities, and revenue and gross profit delivered by predictive campaigns. As long as the team is focused on fixing one problem and has pulled in the right team members and data to address it, they'll see improvements in their chosen metrics. Now we'll talk about how to actually get all the data right.

4. Get the Data Right

As we discussed in earlier chapters, most companies will never have perfectly clean data sets—to steal a phrase that's been heavily overused with regard to investing, that's the unicorn, a mythical creature. Perhaps your efforts to become more data-driven in your marketing and sales are frustrated or stymied by data issues. You might be in the midst of a data cleanup effort with IT and new system architectures that seems never-ending. You might be struggling with null values in your data or poor linkages between data sources, such as marketing, sales, and transaction data. The reality is that no organization's data is perfect, nor even as good as many within the organization might like it to be.

The good news is that you can still put the data that you do have to good use. In fact, we'd contend that the cost of messy data is far lower than you might think, and certainly far lower than the cost of doing nothing (as we discussed in Chapter 4). To illustrate this point, we took the data that we used to build a conversion model for a Fortune 1000 software company and removed half of the successful conversions, effectively simulating the messy and incomplete data that we often see in our customers' databases. While the model quality did decline slightly, Lattice's Predictive Insights Platform was still able to provide significant value, by predicting roughly 60 percent of the conversions in the top 20 percent of the leads.

So what do we mean by "get the data right"? While the magnitude of data is important, it is equally, if not more, important to (1) ensure your training data matches your use-case and (2) apply your model to the right universe of records.

For example, one of our high-growth technology customers decided to build a model that would identify look-alike accounts of customers who had spent more than $200,000 in annual contract value (ACV). With 50,000 accounts in their CRM database, we had to decide how to cut this broader account universe down into the correct positive and negative universes. The positive universe became all customers that had spent more than $200,000 ACV, and the negative universe became all other accounts in the database (whether they were prospects or customers spending less than $200,000).

The model we built had an amazing performance curve. And yet, the insights just weren't all that interesting. The model showed that any companies with very high revenue and very high employee counts were likely to spend more. This came as no surprise to sales leaders who wanted to use this model to build a target account program.

How could we make the model more interesting? What were we really trying to prioritize? We engaged in more discovery for the use-case and went back to the drawing board. We realized that our carefully thought-out training set actually did not match our use-case. We discovered that the sales team was already targeting enterprise accounts—they just had too many of them to target! Based on this knowledge, we revised both our positive and negative event universes to focus only on companies with revenue of $500 million and above. The positive and negative universes were both cut down to include only companies with $500M+ in revenue. This meant that the model would recognize *all* accounts as having high revenue, and therefore not choose revenue as a differentiator for those that spent more. This tweak allowed the training set to align with the use-case: How do we prioritize our enterprise accounts?

This is where data can be tricky. This model was great and helped prioritize a certain set for outreach. However, our customer couldn't use this model against their entire database, because it was specifically built for companies that had over $500 million in revenue. That's the second part of getting the data right—only apply models to the right universe so that you're using the right data in the correct manner and obtaining accurate outcomes.

Many customers ask then, how do I know whether I'm applying it to the right universe? The best way to know is to look at scoring distribution and a percentiles graph. This scoring distribution is stack-ranked, so you should have relatively similar amounts across the board. If you have 70 percent of your leads scoring 90 or above

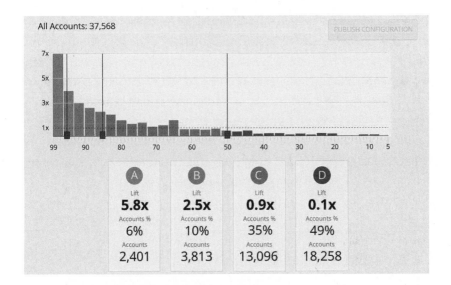

Figure 7.5   Scored Set of Training Data

on a scale of 1 to 99, then you'll know something is amiss. This is why Lattice simultaneously builds a rating engine (Figure 7.5) that shows the distribution of your training set scored against the specific model. Because the training set is representative of the records for your use-case, the ultimate distribution of scores/ratings in your database should not vary greatly from this chart. If your model distribution is wildly different, go work with your AI vendor and ensure that you solve this issue before moving on to the next step.

5. Invest in Training

Many teams underestimate the importance of training their teams to understand and use the predictive insights provided by AI platforms like Lattice. Two types of training need to take place. The first is for the marketing teams or operational teams that manage the platform and will lead the creation of models, segments, and campaign messaging. The second is for the sales reps who are utilizing the insights provided by an AI platform. They need to be able to read, understand, and use the insights provided by the AI platform.

For the operational teams, it's critical that the project manager determine who needs to be trained initially to get the program up and running and that all participate in early training. At Lattice we've seen that training over multiple sessions can cause teams to lose focus and for some people to end up only half-trained. For this reason, we kick off new implementations for our customers with a Launch Workshop, a one-day on-site event during which we coordinate all training needed to launch the initial use-case. Customers leave this session having built the foundation of an AI deployment, including:

- API connections to Lattice products and data workflows
- An initial validation of internal data
- A list of starter campaigns to recognize value quickly

These in-person sessions reduce internal friction to go-live goals by speeding up the implementation of, and vastly improving the quality of, our AI-driven solutions. After the launch marketers and operational team members are ready to start putting AI programs into place. Obviously, our customer success team is always on hand for follow-up questions, but we've found that those teams that invest a whole day with our implementation program see the most early successes.

On the sales side, it's less about how to use the platform itself and more about understanding the importance of the predictive insights. Predictive program leads should spend time with their sales managers on-site, providing hands-on guidance and achieving buy-in, as these managers will be responsible for training and coaching of sales reps. Contrary to what one might expect, the result of this training program should not be a comprehensive how-to guide for a predictive tool but rather a good discussion on why predictive methods are important for the company and how they fit into the sales team's culture and workflow. Since a transition to predictive selling impacts the entire selling cycle, inserting data-driven habits into day-to-day tasks is one of the key areas for your team leaders to focus on in the beginning. Explaining this and getting them onboard is key.

Now your team is ready to launch your predictive platform and start reaping the benefits. But it's important to establish early just how often you'll reassess projects and programs.

6. Use an Agile Method to Fine-Tune Your Plan

Today it's imperative that your team be able to respond rapidly to new inputs or information. Many teams used to make annual plans and never deviate, but a predictive platform can help them recognize when they need to focus on something new or when an external event requires them to shift priorities.

One of the best ways to set a team up to be responsive is to use the agile marketing method. Scott Brinker wrote *Hacking Marketing: Agile Practices to Make Marketing Smarter, Faster, and More Innovative* (Wiley, 2016) and pioneered a way for marketers to utilize the short "sprints" of work that engineering and product teams have utilized for years.

How does Brinker define agile marketing? Simply put, it is the application of scrum-inspired agile software development practices to the management of marketing initiatives. Agile marketers can utilize a number of agile elements, including:

- *Team size and structure.* A team of no more than eight to ten members led by a "scrum master" who facilitates the process
- *The sprint/scrum cycle.* An iterative cycle typically lasting one to four weeks during which the team focuses on a clearly defined and cohesive set of small tasks
- *Process artifacts.* Old school or software tools (from physical whiteboards to digital options like Trello) for managing task prioritization and tracking
- *Philosophy.* A mindset that puts a strong focus on adaptability, prioritization, transparency, responsiveness, empowerment, and experimentation

For some teams this may seem like a no-brainer, but for many it's contrary to the way they plan long-term programs. However, the two methods can coexist as long as teams are willing to put in the planning time in advance.

For example, with a predictive rollout it's important that the team have a phase 1 use-case and know what it will entail from a people, content, and processes standpoint. They should also have high-level plans for what phases 2 and 3 will be, and when they can expect to roll those out. Then they can break phase 1 into smaller chunks that can be bucketed into four-week sprints. For example, the first sprint would focus on getting the data and model ready, while the content, digital, and SDR teams would be preparing the proper content and cadence for campaigns they'd begin running against their first set of predictive prospects. Then the second sprint would entail actually running the campaigns, measuring them, and repeating.

This method is critical because it enables teams to adapt quickly when new information is available. Imagine that the second sprint showed that the email campaigns were working great, but advertising campaigns were performing even worse than before. The operations and digital teams must quickly sit down and discover what went wrong. Then they can make changes and test new programs. Rather than being a fire drill, this process is natural and iterative.

Now that the team is completely prepared, it's time to launch your first predictive program.

7. Start Small, but Launch Big

We talked earlier about starting with one use-case and doing A/B testing to ensure that models and data are correct. That doesn't mean that the program should only be used by a few reps to see how it goes. When you commit to changing one part of your revenue funnel process, the entire team has to be committed to taking full advantage of the new insights that will be available. This goes back to Step 1 in this process: all of the stakeholders must be committed to this new program.

Let's assume that the use-case you've launched with is prioritizing the existing leads in your database, as well as any new ones that come in from various inbound marketing campaigns. Instead of performing an A/B test on a small subset of these leads, it's crucial to assign all leads as either A or B. A small segment of the leads will show results and enable you to measure success metrics, but it will not have a significant impact on your bottom line, because you are using only part of the funnel.

Our most successful customers put a lot of emphasis on achieving a balance between hitting activity targets and preserving quality of execution at the same time. Teams should use predictive tools strategically, as opposed to transactionally. The team shouldn't just be task-oriented or prioritize basic activity metrics and ignore the overall quality of their engagement with customers, that is, they should not focus on checking off as many predictive campaign recommendations as possible during a short timeframe without really investing time and effort into engaging with customers and prospects.

When the entire team is behind the launch of these kinds of programs, the initial sprint with an A/B test can showcase just how powerful predictive insights can be (Figure 7.6). When teams and reps see just how much improvement predictive insights can provide, they'll all begin adopting these practices. If your team only has a quarter of the reps using these new programs and learning new strategies, the successes will not seem as astronomical and adoption rates will stall.

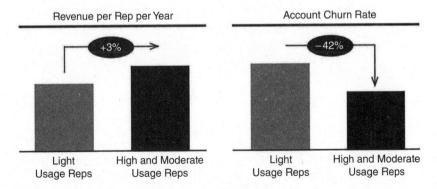

Figure 7.6   Sample Results Against Revenue and Churn Rate

8. Share Early Successes

It's important to share early successes, so that teams will adopt the new tool more quickly. It's normal to want to wait for a huge success before you begin singing the praises of your new AI platform, but for a successful deployment the best way to drive adoption is for all the participating teams to see quick successes. Discussing the small wins can help members of the team who aren't as committed understand that they could also benefit.

For example, a payments processor that Lattice works with started a pilot whereby they began prioritizing their inbound leads for all sales outreach—both SDRs and field reps. The marketing team that was spearheading the pilot provided monthly updates to the sales team showing how much faster the A and B leads were converting into opportunities than the C and D leads were. It would have been easy for the marketing team to wait until they began seeing actual revenue dollars to celebrate the success of the program, but with their long sales cycles they knew they'd lose momentum by waiting that long. Instead, they highlighted, and celebrated, the small successes they saw in their leading indicators, which illustrated how predictive insights were going to impact revenue in the future.

Not only did the marketing team show the value of the information they were providing to Sales, and thus create goodwill, but sales reps were encouraged and more willing to try out the new processes. For something like AI platforms that are more complex than many other technologies, it's critical that early successes be shared broadly to encourage adoption. This is the only way that an organization can realize the true power of predictive analytics.

9. Share Metrics in Weekly Meetings

Implementing an AI platform is an important step in becoming a truly data-driven revenue organization. Once sales and marketing teams are working from the same data sets, conversations around revenue and growth become much more insightful and transparent because the same terminology/data are used.

Because of this, metrics around a predictive program should be discussed in weekly meetings. This is similar to celebrating early victories, but it's also important to acknowledge missteps or issues before they become a problem. Making a habit of including data-driven metrics in weekly meetings establishes a new baseline for how the two teams work together and measure/evaluate their success.

10. Take a Staged Approach

As we mentioned at the beginning of this chapter, the most successful deployments roll out in phases. AI platforms are complex and it's important to work through any issues in one area before pushing into new sections of the business or parts of the revenue funnel.

A major Fortune 1000 company focuses on tax and accounting software. They are a great example of how to do a staged rollout. The business unit has been a Lattice customer for many years, and our platform successfully enabled their team to improve retention and cross-selling opportunities. With our platform they identified super users that had heavy product usage, and worked with those team members to build up adoption of their accounting software in their organization, thereby making the product more sticky and increasing their retention rates.

After a few years of using Lattice in this area successfully, the marketing team at this customer began looking into new ways to utilize the predictive insights they were already generating. They bucketed out the various programs and departments that could benefit from AI (Figure 7.7), and began slowing rolling out new campaigns for which they had predictive insights. Now their outbound sales team is starting to utilize Lattice's scoring and insights to support call prep, while their marketing teams are implementing customized nurture campaigns based on the data enrichments provided by Lattice.

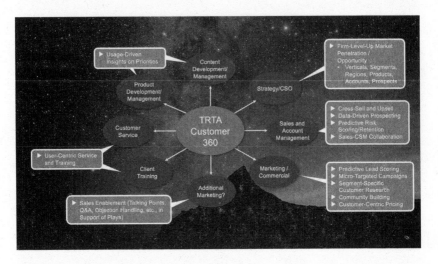

Figure 7.7   360-Degree Customer View

Conclusion

Clearly, implementing an AI platform is not a simple "set it and forget it" technology purchase. It takes time and manpower to determine the best way to generate insights and integrate them into your established workflow. And it also takes the willingness of team members to adopt new processes and learn how to implement them. This is no small task, and those vendors that try to sell a quick AI deployment should be avoided like the plague.

However, teams that dedicate the right resources to new AI programs and invest the time to ensure their first use-case is working properly can completely change the way their company finds new prospects, prioritize their marketing efforts, and increase customer lifetime value. Those companies we've worked with that put in the effort have been rewarded with metrics like a 300 percent increase in conversions, 35 percent higher deal sizes, and 20 percent higher retention. As we mentioned earlier, predictive platforms have the power to impact every section of the revenue funnel positively. Teams that follow these steps for their implementation will harness the power of AI and see their companies' revenue numbers start to skyrocket.

Start Now

As the saying goes, a journey of a thousand miles begins with a single step. While your data may be getting cleaner, it will never be perfect, and there's no time like the present to start using your data to make better decisions. As your data improves, so can your program.

8

Supporting the CMO's Journey

As we discussed at the beginning of this book, CMOs are being put under intense pressure to contribute in a quantifiable manner to the bottom line, without being given any additional resources. This has caused teams to look for ways to target their campaigns more closely and has ushered in the era of ABM.

We believe most companies have been doing some sort of account-centric marketing for years. However, their efforts have been targeted at their top fifty to one hundred accounts because of the resources required for selecting target accounts, researching their key challenges, developing customized offers, and driving campaigns in a coordinated way between sales and marketing. But with the advances in analytics and AI platforms, it is now becoming possible to create segmented, targeted campaigns for a much larger group of accounts.

This has flipped the marketing industry a bit on its side. Suddenly, all marketers were talking about doing ABM and using data points like the one in Figure 8.1 to justify spending money on new ABM-centric technology tools.

The problem with this approach is that many companies were just following the trend, rather than strategically determining how

marketers say ABM strategies outperform other marketing investments on ROI

ITSMA

marketers achieved higher ROI with ABM than with other marketing initiatives

Alltera

marketers say ABM is a must-have strategy for the current B2B marketplace

SiriusDecisions

Figure 8.1   ABM Programs Drive Revenue Success

this new approach would help accelerate revenue. Because there weren't any consistent guidelines around how companies would actually benefit and how to actually execute ABM programs, many companies wasted time talking about ABM, but not actually implementing processes that benefited their particular business use-cases. CMOs were struggling with how to evolve into being account-focused, while still hitting the revenue benchmarks their boards were mandating. That's why our team was inspired to help support the CMO's journey toward ABM success. We realized that there was no discussion around the data required to scale ABM programs successfully beyond those top fifty accounts to the top five hundred and five thousand accounts.

Predictive analytics and AI platforms provide the data and insights needed to execute on the sophisticated segmentation and personalization required for successful ABM programs. This is through several capabilities:

360-Degree View of Prospects and Customers   Predictive analytics platforms give you the ability to look at all the data you already have about your prospects and customers—such as marketing automation, sales interactions in CRM systems, support tickets, transactions, product usages, and more. On top of that, predictive and AI platforms add in external data you may not have about your prospects and customers, such as growth rates, funding information, credit risk data, or technographic data. Predictive analytics platforms combine all your internal and external data, bringing thousands of data points around each prospect and customer together into one clear profile in one platform.

Big Data Processing and Machine Learning With predictive analytics, you can harness the power of big data processing and machine learning to create predictive models for scoring customers and prospects based on how likely they are to buy, what they're likely to buy, and when. You also receive a prioritized list of attributes about your ideal buyer that you can use to enhance your personas.

Ability to Operationalize Insights Finally, predictive analytics platforms make the predictive scores and account-level insights and data available in real-time to your ad platforms, marketing automation systems, and CRM systems so you can drive the right campaigns and end-user experiences.

With the proper data sources and AI platforms in place, CMOs are seeing changes in how their ABM programs are impacting the bottom line. With one single source of customer data, teams are now able to target the right customer, with the right message, at the right time, at scale. And while the advancements in AI platforms have made scalable ABM feasible, they are also benefitting those companies that are focused on leads instead by prioritizing the outreach of revenue teams so they focus their efforts on the best leads. The end result is that all teams are using the same information to target the right people for their business, which is leading to better customer engagement and higher sales volumes for companies that implement these processes and technologies.

Preparing Your Organization for AI

Artificial intelligence (AI) lurks behind consumer applications, often without the end-user's knowledge. From identifying images to recommending friends to serving the right ad, web-scale data has rendered many old algorithms (for example, neural networks) potent and capable of beating humans at similar tasks. But what about Enterprise systems, where the last big wave of intelligence was business intelligence (BI), and it is still playing out twenty years later?

AI is not BI, and the old habits of the Enterprise method, both from the supplier and the buyer side, will need to change before these technologies are widely adopted. With Salesforce's Einstein, Oracle's Intelligent App Cloud, Amazon Machine Learning, and countless other horizontal AI solutions now in the market, it is worth understanding how organizations can extract value from AI.

Business intelligence was the last successful analytics revolution in the Enterprise. When a newly minted data-scientist first encounters BI, her reaction is akin to Groucho Marx commenting on military intelligence. BI systems are built on middle-school math and, although they are very useful, they are not analytically difficult. Middle school math is "horizontal" in that you can apply the basic ideas—summation, averages, deviation, and so forth, to any enterprise without any knowledge of the specifics of the business.

It is no surprise then that the AI solutions from incumbent players have followed the BI playbook. Make a set of standard toolkits available and make the customer responsible for the output of the AI as well as the business outcome of the deployment. But this approach does not work.

Our company, Lattice, built an AI-based marketing and sales solution from the ground up. We first introduced an AI-based cross-sell/up-sell recommender for B2B sales and marketing in 2010. Since then we have expanded our solution to include a number of other use-cases, including finding new prospects, serving targeted ads, outbounding to key accounts, scoring leads, and retaining customers. Along the way we have also deployed our solution more than two hundred times, usually at companies ranging from high-growth mid-market to dozens of Fortune 500 companies. Through the course of engaging with the end-users and continuously refining our solutions, we have learned five important lessons about creating measurable value for our customers.

1. **AI applications need cross-platform data.** Peter Norvig pointed out several years ago (https://www.computer.org/csdl/mags/ex/2009/02/mex2009020008-abs.html) that mediocre algorithms with more data beat great algorithms with less data. Therefore, AI applications that limit themselves to a single platform will invariably be beaten by applications that can make use of cross-platform data as well as web-scale data. For example, at Lattice we have built a global index of over 250M businesses that we track for changes and events using web-based and offline signals. Each of these signals is fed into predictions of future purchases. For 90 percent of our deployments, these "external signals" are much better predictors than signals derived from CRM or marketing automation alone.

2. **End-users need explanations, not orders.** A sales rep is never satisfied with purchase probability because it is not actionable information. She wants to know why the score is what it is, why this account was picked over others, and what she should talk about when she calls the account. The recent surge in AI was caused by the spectacular success of one particular method—deep learning. Deep learning–based AI is ideally suited for high-dimensional problems, for example, image recognition, but it doesn't explain its rationale in a form understandable by humans. Any AI will have to explain itself to end-users or lose their trust—this limits the usefulness of deep learning–based AI to sales and marketing problems.

3. **Data scientists need controls.** While an end-user may be satisfied with a score and an explanation, the data scientists in

the organization will want full control. Black box algorithms may work in the SMB segment but don't work as well in the Enterprise. In fact, our platform took a giant step forward when we opened it up so that data scientists could use their own algorithms on our data. AI is supposed to amplify human intelligence, not replace it.

4. **AI has to be right.** Neils Bohr—a contemporary of Albert Einstein—famously said, "It's very hard to make predictions, especially about the future." Unlike the BI world in which the analysis is focused on understanding the past, AI applications have to outperform human guesses about the future. At Lattice, we take responsibility for the quality of predictions, not just the quality of software. We monitor every model in production at every customer through a set of automated tests. Any drift in models is detected automatically, and alerts are sent out to the customer success team. This would require a massive change for traditional BI vendors who just have to deliver bug-free code that can do middle-school math. Will their predictions be as accurate for a $1,000 product being sold through the channel as for a $100,000 product being sold direct? "One size fits all" does not work for AI applications.

5. **The vendor is responsible for the business outcome.** Rob Bernshteyn, the CEO of Coupa, has pointed out the secular trend from SaaS (software as a service) to VaaS (value as a service). Nowhere is this trend clearer than in the world of AI applications. We have learned through experience that aligning closely with the business process, embedding the solution deeply into the workflow, and being responsible for the outcome are the only ways to successfully deliver AI. The BI vendor model of dropping the software, having an SI integrate it, and making it the business's responsibility to derive value does not work anymore.

At the end of the day, accelerating revenue in today's B2B world is incredibly difficult. CMOs are faced with a shifting landscape of technologies, while at the same time they're being handed more and more responsibility for the revenue pipeline. In order for them to succeed in this new world of analytic-driven marketing, we believe CMOs need to implement AI and predictive analytics platforms so they can bring marketing toward a true 1-to-1 conversation between a company and a customer.

Appendix
Buyers Guide to AI and Predictive Platforms

WHEN MAKING ANY technology investment that promises great returns, it is critical that organizations carefully vet their options. As you evaluate platforms that will provide your team with AI and predictive insights to improve your marketing and sales efforts, your organization should seek a partner and a solution that best reduce risk and can maximize results.

Several key criteria must be evaluated in order to ensure you're picking the right platform for your particular business use-cases. In this appendix, we've laid out the thirteen key criteria to consider and provided a breakdown of what kinds of questions you should ask a partner before selecting your AI platform.

1. Data Quality
2. Data Breadth
3. Data Integration
4. Sales Interface
5. Enterprise Security
6. Transparency
7. Self-Service Modeling
8. Unlimited Modeling

9. Use-Case Flexibility
10. Real-Time Scoring
11. Customer Success Reputation
12. Track Record of Success
13. Vendor Viability

This is meant to be a checklist for your team, so under each criterion we outline why this particular element is important and provide specific questions that you should ask a partner and provide details on why these questions are critical. This should help guide your process as you choose the appropriate AI platform partner to help you accelerate revenue across all teams.

1. Data Quality

An AI platform should score and segment customers prospects using a combination of internal data and external data. Data quality refers to the completeness and accuracy of this data. Completeness means: "Can my AI partner 'match' external data to all of my customers and prospects, both in the United States and globally?" Accuracy means: "Is the external data that my predictive partner provides accurate—for example, does the industry designation match the actual value?"

Why is this important? It's because AI algorithms are accurate only when they are informed by reliable, high-fidelity data.

Questions to Ask

- Ask the potential partners to provide a list of all companies headquartered in a metro area that the partner is tracking. You can select a certain employer type (e.g., 100 to 1,000 employees) to simplify the evaluation.
  - Inspect the list to determine: (1) Which partner tracks the most companies? (2) Which partner has accurate data (when comparing fields like "industry" and "employees"?

2. Data Breadth

Any AI platform that is focused on improving marketing and sales outcomes will score customers and prospects using external data that provides a more holistic view of the business, the technologies they use today, and the business changes they are facing. Data breadth refers to attributes such as: "Cloud Maturity" or "Public Cloud Provider" that might be important for your company.

Why is this important? An AI algorithm or predictive score is only accurate when it is informed by reliable, high-fidelity data about characteristics that matter specifically to your business.

Questions to Ask

- Ask the potential partners to provide a profile of what kind of attributes are tracked for accounts.
- Ask the potential partners to provide a list of the specific attributes that are relevant to your business that can be tracked.

3. Data Integration

Data integration refers to the ability of your AI platform to leverage every available data signal from within your enterprise.

Why is this important? Your business may have a variety of service models—including new offerings that charge customers for service based on the intensity of their usage. To score accurately for purchase likelihood and customer value, a solution must include more than "transactions," it also needs to include any relevant data about product usage, customer behavior, and so forth.

Questions to Ask

- Ask the potential partners how they expect you to provide an ongoing stream of data from "product usage" or other internal systems. Many vendors will require you to load data every time a predictive model is built, which will reduce your agility.

- Ask your AI partners whether they are able to accept streaming data for automatic incorporation into algorithms and segments.
- Ask the potential partners whether they are able to accept data from a variety of sources, such as marketing automation platforms, CRM systems, ERP systems, product usage tracking, and others.

4. Sales Interface

A high-level AI platform for marketing and sales will push scores to sales people though a platform like Salesforce.com. Whatever sales interface your company uses should be integrated with your AI platform so sales reps can view information about a given lead or account in their day-to-day workflow.

Why is this important? An AI platform will generate maximum value only if it provides sales with clear, coherent, business-centric rationales that explain why they should engage a given lead or account.

Questions to Ask

- Ask potential partners to demonstrate their sales interface to your sales reps.
- Ask sales reps which interface is the most compelling and intuitive.

5. Enterprise Security

Any AI platform will leverage your customer data—including customer names, marketing response activity, and transactions. All of this data should be carefully secured; in some instances it is heavily regulated.

Why is this important? Your customers' data is a critical and confidential business asset. Mismanagement of customer data or accidental disclosure due to security holes would permanently and significantly impact your customers' trust in you.

Questions to Ask

- Ask potential partners to provide two security attestations:
  - (1) Security Attestation for Hosting Environment. The environment must be ISO-27001 compliant.
  - (2) Security Attestation for Data Management Practices. The partner is subject to annual audits from third parties to validate data management practices.

Be especially careful with your vendor responses here as some will play games. They may claim, for example: "We utilize Amazon Web Services for hosting, which is ISO 27001 security certified." This is analogous to claiming, "I own a Volvo, so I'm a safe driver." Unless the platform itself is certified, your customer data is still at risk.

6. Transparency

An AI platform uses algorithms to score leads, customers, and prospects. The scores constitute many factors. Transparency refers to the ability of marketers and sales reps to see why each score was created.

Why is this important? Many AI and predictive solutions are "black box" and don't provide any details about how a score or insight is generated. Your team members will want to understand *why* each score was created to validate accuracy of predictions. Additionally, sales reps will only adopt the solution if they trust the predictive scores produced by the system. Showing team members an easy-to-understand rationale behind the scores is key to driving adoption, in our experience.

Questions to Ask

- Ask potential partners to show you how their product tells the marketing and sales departments why a score was created.
- Ask potential partners to show how they leverage transparency to help ensure adoption of the solution by sales.

7. Self-Service Modeling

An AI platform will be used by your marketing operations and demand generation teams to create predictive models, score leads, prioritize accounts, and so forth. Your team will want to be self-sufficient—not reliant on a partner's team to do the work quickly.

Why is this important? Many AI and predictive companies have analysts build predictive models on behalf of their customers. Rather than feel "beholden" to the analyst or data science team's schedule and availability, you want the agility that comes from being able to build predictive models entirely on your own.

Question to Ask

- Ask the potential partners whether their solutions give you the ability to create a predictive model entirely on your own.

8. Unlimited Modeling

An AI platform must allow for the ability to create as many predictive models as needed for your business.

Why is this important? Different products, geographies, and business segments need different predictive models so that they can more accurately predict, enrich, and execute targeted marketing campaigns and sales plays. This is especially important for enterprises that have multiple product lines and operate internationally.

Questions to Ask

- Ask your potential partners to provide examples of their customers using different models for their predictive programs.

9. Use-Case Flexibility

You will use an AI platform to score leads, identify cross-selling opportunities, highlight capacity expansion opportunities for the same products, and predict the next best offer for a particular account.

Why is this important? Many AI solutions score leads or accounts only, but have no mechanism for finding expansion opportunities for your existing accounts. Companies with a large install base often rely on driving cross-sell/up-sell as a lever of business growth. The vendor you choose needs the ability to enrich and identify opportunities for cross-sell programs as well as the ability to focus on finding net-new accounts.

Questions to Ask

- Ask potential partners to describe internal data sources that can be leveraged for cross-sell.
- Ask potential partners what types of models may be created (such as cross-sell or retention).

10. Real-Time Scoring and Enrichment

You will use an AI platform to score and enrich the details of prospects and customers as they "raise their hands."

Why is this important? Real-time scoring is necessary if you want timely sales follow-up from the "hand-raisers." The odds of qualifying a lead drop by a factor of six unless an inbound lead is called within an hour, according to a study by InsideSales.com on lead response management.

Questions to Ask

- Ask potential partners to provide customer examples of how they are using real-time scoring in production.
- Ask potential partners to show that they can use their systems to score leads within a specific time-period.

11. Customer Success Reputation

There is a wide discrepancy in the quality of customer success teams—some are consultative and have a reputation for effective enablement and training, while others are able to install basic software but provide almost no useful training or advisory services.

Why is this important? It can be challenging to install a new AI platform and then enforce the cultural changes that drive success from such initiatives. You want a partner who will guide your success along the way, starting with a seamless integration and then offering continuing education on best practices or new use-cases that the AI platform can address.

Questions to Ask

- Tell potential partners you want to meet the actual team that will work with you.
- Ensure the team is geographically located in a time zone that works with your team's requirements.

12. Track Record of Success

The experience of peer companies that have been using an AI platform in production for more than one year is important for understanding which solutions create measurable value for their customers.

Why is this important? Your company wants to realize a measurable increase in key sales and marketing metrics, such as "revenue per rep" and "conversion rate per campaign."

Questions to Ask

- Ask for the number of customers with more than one year of deployment, not just a total number of customers, as some vendors include free trials and pilots as customers in their claims.
- Ask for contact information at more than two peer companies (same industry, same size) that have been using the software in production for more than a year.

13. Vendor Viability

Many companies claim they have a predictive solution or have an AI-based offering, but are not viable in terms of funding, revenue, or customer traction.

Why is this important? As with most hot technology areas, many companies have recently entered the field. A lot of those companies will quickly disappear from the space. It is imperative that you select partners who will be around in the long run.

Questions to Ask

- Ask how long the vendor has been in business as an AI and predictive platform.
- Ask how many employees the vendor has.
- Ask what VCs are backing the vendor, as VCs do a tremendous amount of research before making an investment?
- Ask how much VC funding has the vendor received?

Index

Page references followed by *fig* indicate an illustrated figure; followed by *t* indicate a table.

A

A/B testing model for programs, 139*fig*, 146–147

ABM (account-based marketing): "ABM Programs Drive Revenue Success" argument for, 153–154*fig*; benefits of, 19, 153; comparing traditional and, 17; data as the foundation for, 31–59; description of, 12–13; determining if Sales and Marketing teams should use, 109; how it brings marketers closer to 1:1 marketing, 57–59; lessons learned on building AI-based marketing/sales solution and, 156–158; potential for marketing solutions using, 14–15; SiriusDecisions' definition of, 19; supporting CMO's journey toward adopting, 153–159. *See also* AI (artificial intelligence); B2B marketing; Predictive marketing

ABM data foundation: common pitfalls of, 51–57; five steps in building a, 32–50*t*; importance of building a robust, 31; quality of contact data as part of the, 57–59. *See also* Customer database

ABM data foundation steps: 1. bound project objectives/scope with available data, 32–38*fig*; 2. consolidate and align historic data, 32, 38–39; 3. build creative segments and audiences using AI, 32, 39–45; 4. execute campaigns against AI-assisted segments/audiences, 32, 45–47; 5: measure results using metrics, 32, 48–50*t*

ABM program strategies: create relevant messages and content, 21, 24–25; execute tactics for conversion, 21, 25–27*fig*; measure impact, 21, 28; summary of key points, 22*fig*; target your high-value accounts, 21, 22–23

ABM programs: enable front-line sales performance management, 28; evaluate performance of your, 28; strategies to use for, 21, 22*fig*–28

ABM projects: build creative segments and audiences using AI, 39–45; common pitfalls in, 51–57; decide on process step and execution channel, 36, 38; define a target event for, 33–35; measure results on revenue,

171